# Changing Faces

*Stories of Death and Resurrection*

# Changing Faces

*Stories of Death and Resurrection*

Brian Mountford

MOWBRAY

First published 1990 by **Mowbray**
A Cassell imprint
Artillery House, Artillery Row, London SW1P 1RT, England

**British Library Cataloguing in Publication Data**
Mountford, Brian
   Changing faces: stories of death and resurrection.
   1. Death – Christian viewpoints
   I. Title
   248.4

ISBN 0–264–67198–8

Phototypeset by Input Typesetting Ltd, London
Printed and bound in Great Britain by
Biddles Ltd, Guildford and King's Lynn

# Foreword

There is a lot of talk both here and in the USA at the moment about 'narrative theology' and the theology of 'personal experience', the need for both imagination and personal openness, and a lot of books are produced about how this is essential, but nobody actually *does* it. It seems to me that this is what Brian Mountford is attempting. And with a high degree of success.

These pieces – and it is difficult to know quite what else to call them: they are somewhere between stories, meditations and sermons – offer us something genuinely distinctive and original. Here you will find a kind of 'liberal' theology which is framed within the authentic Christian tradition and which is truly liberal – is open-ended and not self-righteous. Here you will also meet a writer who is prepared to use his personal life, with its doubts and difficulties, as the material for exploration and thought.

This is not a book for those who want the treacled certainties of socially conventional piety. It is a book for people who want to read and think about ultimate values, but find they can't enjoy the complex discourse of much contemporary theology. It is a book for people who think that creativity and laughter and dailiness, as well as thoughtfulness, love and sadness, are important parts of their life, and God's.

*Sara Maitland*

# Contents

# Acknowledgements

J. M. Dent & Sons for permission to quote from Ignazio Silone, *Fontamara*, translated by Eric Mosbacher (1986)

André Deutsch Limited for permission to quote from Peter Shaffer, *Amadeus* (1980), and Dan Jacobson, *Her Story* (1988)

Faber and Faber for permission to quote from 'A Taste for Truth' from Anne Ridler, *New and Selected Poems* (1988)

William Heinemann for permission to quote from Graham Swift, *Waterland* (1983)

Oxford University Press for permission to quote from Rudoph Otto, *The Idea of the Holy*, translated by J. W. Harvey (2nd ed. 1950)

*To*
*Annette*
*Zoe and Charlotte*

# Nellie

Today I went to visit Miss Templeman. She lives in the almshouses. Actually, lives is hardly the word – exists, maybe. Or sits. Yes, Miss Templeman who sits in our almshouses from getting up at five-thirty in the morning to going to bed at eight at night. If sitting were your vocation you would at least expect to practise it in a well-upholstered chair, but this particular nonagenarian passes her days in an aluminium-framed garden chair, with bright orange, green and yellow stripes that conjure up the salt breezes, seaside rock, and Punch and Judy shows. The other furnishings are sparse: a kitchen table with two pine chairs, a 'utility' plywood coffee table covered by a purple hand-knitted cloth, and a built-in dresser displaying remarkably few clues to the past – plain cups, saucers, plates, a coloured glass vase, pension book and medical card. The impression is not one of poverty but of complete simplicity, an anchoress's cell, with the only hint of comfort in the hospitable sprung seat of the visitor's chair.

I cycled along the path that skirts the cricket ground from the church to Balaam's Lane, being careful to avoid a puncture from the hawthorn cuttings left by the Council last time they trimmed the hedge. The red-brick gabled facade of the almshouses looks out over the cricket field with the self-satisfied dignity of a middle-class villa. In fact the building comprises six tenements erected in 1894 by public subscription in memory of a long-serving vicar who had prudently married the squire's daughter. Each unit has one upstairs and one downstairs room, connected by a boxed staircase that protrudes into the living-room, but opens directly into the bedroom, which is consequently well-proportioned and spacious, with a chimney breast in the centre of one wall, enhanced by a black iron fireplace and mantelpiece. This upper room overlooks a unique suburban

1

landscape – a slice of rural England plonked down in the middle of North London. In the distance, framed by historic oaks, rises the church, Victorian Early English, like a mini-cathedral, and stretching before it fifty acres of cricket fields, partially wooded, and not a single semi to spoil the illusion.

The tenements are for aged or infirm poor over the age of fifty-five years, to keep them from the workhouse. There are no bathrooms, and a lean-to extension to the ground floor provides a scullery kitchen with adjacent toilet. Miss Templeman cooks on two gas rings, the apertures of which are clogged up with the greasy remnants of forgotten meals, so that the yellow flames jump and gasp for gas. She washes her clothes, her crockery, and her face in a shallow stoneware sink, tea-stain brown and cabbage smelly.

Naturally the social services have done their best, sorting out a home-help on Tuesdays and Thursdays, and arranging for meals-on-wheels, but Miss Templeman cherishes her independence, likes things as they are, dislikes improvements. Even when the trustees installed central heating she was reluctant to accept it, not liking the disturbance, and fearing that as a result she would be more prone to colds and winter bugs. It is as if the symbols of the present destroy her sense of solidarity and continuity with the past: no television, no telephone, no frozen food, no new-fangled pills. She is a time capsule, one of the last Victorians, seven years older than the building she sits in, which has itself for nearly forty years been noted as a historical monument in the local history of this suburb.

I knocked, lifted the latch, and walked in. Following a well-established ritual, Miss Templeman was lost for words, but smiled deeply, as if her sculptor had gone too far with the chisel, and with remarkable mimetic skill she acts that she is honoured and unworthy to receive my visit. She motions towards the visitor's chair, and I take off my anorak with exaggerated informality and bung it on the table, trying to release the dramatic tension. We both sit down, the old lady's hand remaining outstretched towards my chair until I speak. 'How have you been this week? Has your nephew been to see you? Have you been getting on with your knitting?'

Silently, mysteriously, she sits gazing at me, patient and interrogative. I am not sure whether she can see me or how

I appear to her, because one eye is completely blurred by a cataract, and although she has had an operation on the other, her glasses are usually spattered with dust and fat and other tiny particles of debris. I start again. 'I think there'll be a frost tonight; it's very clear and the wind is in the north.' (It always seems to be winter when I visit.) She ignores my trivial meteorological observations, and her face changes from benign enigma to furrowed gloom.

'It's no good, Vicar, it's no good. There's something wrong. I thought you could help me, but you can't.'

'What's wrong? Can you put your finger on it?'

'No. That's the whole point. It's no good. It must be something in the church . . . perhaps I should stop coming to church . . . but there again . . .'

'But you enjoy coming to church.'

'Ah! Yes, but I shouldn't enjoy coming to church, should I. There, you see, the *church* is my downfall', she said with a note of triumph.

'I'm sorry, I just can't understand how the church can cause you so much distress', I said.

'It's all wrong. Pride comes before a fall, so to say. I know my place and I'm out of place there, aren't I. I shouldn't be there . . . but there again . . .'

And so we go on teasing out the obsessions in circular and irrational conversations; the old woman's Victorian notion that church-going is for the gentry, and that by attending the service in her maroon hat and gloves she is stepping beyond her station, putting on airs and graces that perhaps friends and relations long since dead would have mocked her for. She wants to say too that she is miserably alone and that there is no end in sight to her isolation which stretches across the days and merges into months, seasons, years, until these very frames which shape our lives have no meaning. Only death can put her days into perspective, but, as she says, she is too fit and healthy to die.

'Oh, it's no good, Vicar.'

And is there something else? Is there another unspeakable emotion apart from the feeling of social inferiority and aching loneliness? Does she feel guilty because she is in love with a clergyman? 'Oh, Vicar, you must always keep me in thy presence near. Our spirits are one . . . I know you are with me . . . but, no, I mustn't. I'm a silly old woman', she says, clothing infatuation with spiritual cliché. She is uncertain whether I have understood the riddle, and I make no attempt to enlighten her. I do not deny or affirm what she has said, and we seem to get on very well. We rarely talk of anything else but these obsessions which are reeled out week after week, and mulled over between visits, unless there is some redeeming practical matter to do with the management of the almshouses, or one of the other tenants has had a fall, or attracted rats with food intended for the birds.

But is there more to this old Dame Trot who sits blanketed before one of those infuriatingly insincere electric fires that flicker with unnatural flames? Has she really lost all her memory of the past, as she claims? And did she once see a vision of a priest coming to her across the cricket field on the day of my induction, like John the Baptist emerging from the wilderness of her regret to announce light and love in her last days? She had, besides, now lived in the almshouses for twenty years. She came to die there twenty years ago. This amnesia, this life-forgetting, was such a practical way to stifle life's interminable ordinariness. Or perhaps more accurately her story was untellable because of its dark secret. How mean of me to enjoy her ancient solitude because it was nostalgic like a Christmas card, the poor woman who lived across the snow-covered fields in another century, and was grateful to receive a 50-pence calendar of the church from this yule-tide visitor who reminded her of Harry.

She had let slip about Harry. He was her lover once, when she lived in Finsbury Park and worked as a seamstress in the Euston Road. But that was before the First World War, when she was young and knew the inhibited passion of Edwardian womanhood, desire, and dreaming of babies that she could clothe in the tiny, superbly crafted infant garments that she knitted then and still knits today. Harry's pockets always jangled as he strolled cockily along in his flat cap and waistcoat; it was not with money that they jingled, but they jangled with keys, because he was an apprentice locksmith in Clerkenwell, learning how to cut lock barrels, and do the decorative work which surrounds custom-made locks. To Nellie he was a right jolly roger who made her laugh and skip and feel like spring and forget all about her long beaky nose that had been the tease and taunt of other boys ever since when, at the age of puberty, it had begun

4

to sprout: nosy Nellie, nosy Nellie, they used to cry. Mind
your business or it'll be chopped off. He was her man, and
she would serve him. So once a week she would wash his
white overalls to save him on the laundry bills because he
lived in digs. And on Thursdays she would get his tea for
him, with her mother and sisters, in the house over their
greengrocer's shop in the Seven Sisters Road. It had to be
Thursdays because that was early closing when father went
down to his club to play billiards, and he was a vile-tem-
pered man who disliked having people round. He even gave
the impression of not liking people in his shop, where he'd
grunt in response to their 'Gooddays' and 'Goodmornings',
and look resentful if he had to go out the back to fetch a
special order or replenish the display boxes. The women said
it was a wonder he had any customers at all, but they
excused him on the grounds that he had to get up so early
every morning to go to Covent Garden to buy the fruit and
vegetables, and that as a consequence he was never properly
rested. But you could see the drink hung heavily in his eyes,
and his head ached with it.

On the Thursday in question Harry had surprised his
boss by wearing his best bib and tucker for work, and then
by being late back after the lunch-break, which was
uncharacteristic. He had been to visit an old mate who was
in the jewellery game. Clerkenwell was full of electro-platers,
polishers, gilders, brass-turners, gold-chain makers and silver
beaters, and this mate of Harry's had fixed a nice little ring
of pierced silver with a small emerald, that Harry had
obtained in town, set into it. Safely in his waistcoat pocket,
after work, the ring and Harry clattered along on the tram
to the Seven Sisters Road, where the lad bought a bunch of
anemones (her favourite) from a gypsy girl, and prepared to
propose.

When Nellie raised her hand to see whether the stone
would glitter in the lamplight, the mother and sisters cooed
and hovered, peered and clucked and threw their glances at
Harry, who wagged his head from side to side, confident
and gleeful as he tucked into shepherd's pie. He must stay
tonight to share the news with Mr Templeman when he gets
in, insisted the mother, which seemed to the girls a capital
idea, but Harry's spirit waned. When the old man lurched
in all beery and raw, and Nellie showed her left hand for

admiration, he yelled, 'What's that on your finger you little hussy? I suppose you're in the family way. Get it off at once, and I'll shove it down the throat of him that gave it you. I'll not have you or any daughter of mine marry Harry Knight, not this year or next or the year after that.'

What had turned Templeman against Harry? Did he know something about him that the others did not? Was he a petty burglar, maybe, with all those keys, or a murderer, or what? Was it simply that her father would be jealous of any strutting cockney sparrow that courted Nellie? Eventually the war took Harry. She waved him off from Victoria station where he was to die in the macabre and muddy futility of northern France with half his generation.

After the war her sisters married and soon there were plenty of babies to knit for. 'And when Rachel saw that she bore Jacob no children, Rachel envied her sister; and said unto Jacob, Give me children or else I die. And Jacob's anger was kindled against Rachel: and he said, Am I in God's stead, who hath withheld from thee the fruit of the womb?'

So Miss Templeman came to church to challenge God, and she felt guilty – '. . . it's no good . . . it must be something in the church . . . perhaps I should stop coming to church . . .' Yet it was there, in that Gilbert Scott building that floated for her like an ark across the fields, that she was accepted. The dear old, tired old, naughty old lady who would sit in her pew until she could be escorted out on the arm of the vicar. She was accepted, taken seriously, driven home, visited, prayed for, helped with shopping, listened to in the endless disappointment of her dying, which seemed to stretch as far into the future as it had into the past.

# Close to the Bone

And when he had come out of the boat, there met him
out of the tombs a man with an unclean spirit, who
lived among the tombs. (Mark 5.2)

It was the day Joey smashed the crucifix that my little
daughter brought a bone into church. Look Daddy, what's
this? she asks. But I pretend to be grown up: Please don't
interrupt when I am talking. Is it a bone? It looks like a
bone, Daddy.

She tapped and prodded me in the legs with it. The
person with whom I spoke, more kindly, wants to see it
though. Where did you find that?

Outside.

Outside of the church?

Yes. In the garden.

The service had not long ended and people were milling in
the aisles, taking out diaries, rounding up their young. A
doctor from the congregation was called over. Yes, it was
human, a tibia, an adult tibia. The message spread quickly;
they've found a bone, a human bone. Curiosity and advice
crowded like vultures.

Perhaps we had better call the police.

Has everyone here had their tetanus jab?

A plastic bag. Has someone got a plastic bag? This might
be from an old plague pit. Human remains have been found
here before, Vicar. Pressure on inner-city burial space was
very great in the early nineteenth century.

The gardener has been digging too enthusiastically.
Reluctant laughter.

Wouldn't it be nice if I were to put on my robes and
say some words from the burial service?

It was a human bone she found not a chicken bone, or
a wine bottle, a used hypodermic needle, an old shoe, or

7

any piece of debris left by the people who make their temporary home amongst the tombs of our churchyard. There they sit and swig, talk, roll up fags, plan their campaigns of begging and conning in this city. Well, Father, I've just come down from Newcastle to see a friend, but he's gone away, and now I've got no money to get back. Could you help me out, Father, with the fare? He fumbles in his pockets to produce a dog-eared piece of paper printed with the letterhead of the Department of Health and Social Security, which I may keep as a hostage to fortune and repayment next Friday. I refuse. Well, then, could I spare something for a cup of tea? And in the next few days, with the memory of his face pinned up in my mind like a 'wanted' poster, I see him in conversation around the streets so sincere, so earnest, so disarming – all I need is my fare back to Newcastle. Then one day someone falls for it, and he dances all the way to the off-licence, rejoicing and giving thanks in anticipation of getting smashed out of his brains, and pulling across the curtains to shut out reality.

What was I to do with the bone my daughter found? I couldn't see the point of adding ritual to inconvenience. When our cat was run over last year the children took it badly. They found it by the dustbin stiff and arched out like a feline hurdler, with a trickle of blood from its mouth. I don't like cats and they had spent days talking me into having one. Now it – Webster they had baptised it in the bird-bath – now Webster had got killed on Zoe's birthday. She asked me to bury it in an unmarked place in the garden. She wanted me to hide her sadness in a place where she wouldn't be able to find it. Naturally I chose the vegetable garden in general and the brassica bed in particular, where the fragile remains would quickly rot and feed the brussels sprouts. That is how I'd like to go myself! So I buried the bone beneath the sickliest shrub in the churchyard where slowly it would release its calciferous goodness and find new life in leaf, thorn and stem.

It was later that day that Joey broke the crucifix. My enquiries suggest between the hours of four and five thirty in the afternoon, because the girl on the shop thinks she saw him hanging around just before she went off for her four o'clock tea break, although she couldn't be certain, and when I arrived to get ready for evensong, there was Joey sitting before the votive candle stand and the icons, pleased as Punch and looking rather holy. Then I noticed the unfamiliar vacancy – the figure had been ripped from the cross leaving only the carved white ivory feet and pedestal, attached by an obstinate nail.

The men of the tombs are raw and private; they huddle at one end of the churchyard out of earshot, leaning in upon oath-edged talk, occasionally turning the whites of harassed eyes. Then one will break the circle and stagger behind the cypresses for a piss. His face, anger-red, unshaven, purple-lipped, is gashed with scabs and bruises, caused either by falling when completely smashed, or fighting over a disputed bottle. He reels back adjusting the fly of his stained trousers, glancing quickly to left and right as if some recollection of conventional modesty has suddenly penetrated his thoughts. Then, for no obvious reason, the group rises and moves crablike across the flower bed leaving a trail of litter and compacted earth.

The way to the Radcliffe Camera was cordoned off with the kind of running hurdles that the police use for crowd control.

'What's going on?' I said to the policeman.

'Apparently, some wealthy Japanese guy has given all his books to the Library, and now they're buttering him up.'

Then the new benefactor emerged, beaming his import-ant grin off all the surrounding buildings, like a transmitter signalling to a satellite. Around him were these university types in gowns, furry hoods, and mortar-boards, bowing and scraping, as if to say, have you got any more where that lot came from? And while this ballet is going on, lurching from nowhere, comes this old guy singing 'Itsha long way to Tipperary, Itsha long way to go. Itsha long way to Tipper-ary, to the shweetest girl I know.' Then he holds out his cap to the party, and as they walk forward, the men in furry hoods trying discreetly to shoo him away, he does a Sir Walter Raleigh and walks backwards, bowing with a great flourish, trying all the time to take a collection. He was not so stupid either to miss the ironic humour of what he was doing.

On my way back into church through the churchyard I saw a man of about fifty, small, perky, in cowboy boots, open-neck shirt and red neck-scarf, holding a white stick tap, tap, tapping his way down the steps and along the edge of the kerb which surrounds the grass. The crazy thing was, he could see. 'Don't get yourself all screwed up about me, Guvnor', he chuckled, 'I'm not blind, just practising. I mean you never know when it might happen to you, do you. Everyone ought to have had a bit of practice.'

Yesterday three men, and a woman, with a black-and-white dog encamped in the pews at the back of the church. One was out for the count on a pew, another gave a mournful rendition of 'I belong to Glasgow' on his harmonica, the one with the banjo rocked backwards and forwards swigging from a bottle, and the woman, smiling, watched them both with touching, if baffling, admiration. Irreverent and curious the dog roamed the church, sniffing down the aisles and pews. I spoke to them politely saying that we were unable to allow dogs in the church or the playing of musical instruments, and that food or drink were not permitted to be eaten on the premises, so would they please move on.

Are you telling us to leave the House of God?

I am asking you to respect it.

This is Jesus' house, and we can stay here if we want.

But surely you want to treat his house with respect.

What are we doing wrong? We've just come in to say our prayers, Father. Just to say a few prayers. Will you say a prayer for us please, Father? Meet my wife, Father, says the mouth-organist.

How-do-you-do?

The banjo man lifts his bottle to his lips in defiance.

I'm sorry, I must ask you to go.

And who the fuck do you think you are? asks the banjoist.

I am the priest.

Call yourself a fucking priest. You're scum. You're dirt.

This is God's house.

Do you believe in Jesus, then? Tell us, do you believe in Jesus? You think we're scum, don't you? You think we're dirt. What does Jesus think?

Clumsy and stupid in defeat I suggest that I might call the police. All right. All right. We're going. Call yourself a bloody priest! They stay for a while as I retreat to give them space to leave of their own accord, with a scrap of dishevelled dignity. As they shuffle away the banjoist swears at the top of his voice, cursing the Church and the name of Christ. At the door he takes a handful of hymn-books from the bookcase and hurls them across the floor. The one who is asleep remains supine on the bench and with the caretaker I wake him and move him on. He stinks, and he leaves behind a wet patch from which the urine has trickled down into the joint between the seat and the back of the pew. Inwardly I am grateful for his incontinence because it justifies my action, provides a let-out clause, small print in my version of the imitation of Christ. It is obvious, surely you would agree, that not for all the compassion in the world does it make sense to allow this great church, where Cranmer, Wesley and Newman changed the course of English Church history, to become no better than a stinking urinal. The caretaker, returning with mop and disinfectant, speaks again of resignation if I don't stop this sort of thing happening.

Yes, I understand. I am angry myself. Bewildered and furious in the face of mindless, anarchic chaos. Why do they smash their empty bottles on the concrete bench where they themselves like to sit? Why break glass across the tombstones so that it shatters and splinters into the grass where after church, sometimes in flimsy sandals, my five-year-old likes to hunt for bones? And what was the point of lighting a bonfire in the middle of the lawn when, if they had to do it, they could have used the place where the gardener burns the rubbish? Damn them.

We were made for love. Why else would the God of love form us in his own image? It is he that has given us the gifts of relationship: compassion, understanding, imagination, consciousness, the ability to give, to accept, to honour, to interpret the experiences of the senses, and yet we hide these treasures in a field. Is it because we are afraid of squandering such treasures that we have dug a cavernous pit in the field of compromise and buried them, and in their place invented clichés, short-cuts, prefabrications, parodies of relationship to get by with? The nurse or doctor patronising the patient, party small talk filled with forks and faces, public-bar bonhomie (my shout), the habitual gestures of marriage, the forelock-tugging politeness of the shopkeepers and waiters performing for money, the formalities of court-rooms, board-meetings, classrooms, the attitudes of priests and policemen.

11

We do not *see* each other through these inventions. We were made for love. Oh yes, sure. But we begin to convince ourselves that love is unmanageable in the practical necessities of everyday life. Too much love and instead of saving the world we will bring it to a standstill, on the friction of its own axis. So we pursue the love-ideal like a child chasing after pigeons in the square who knows that they will always flutter away nonchalantly just out of reach. Indeed that is the fun of the game. What would she do if she were to catch one?

But I know I handled it badly my meeting with the mouth-organ man, not acknowledging his humanity, or asking who he was, where he came from, introducing myself, patting the dog, or recognising how on a cold, wet day damp and depression get under the flesh and into the bones and into the marrow of the mind. If we had only begun to know each other then I could have outlined reasonably the ground rules for our relationship. Love is much easier when you know where you stand.

So here I am again, in the same old suit, wearing my guilt unstylishly. It is my guilt that allows me to pass by on the other side. At least I feel guilty. I could be indifferent: well it's their lookout if they choose to live that way. Or ride-a-cock-horse reactionary, denounce them as a menace to society. Parasites. (In a loud voice as if shouting after them.) Dump them out in the countryside each day and make them walk back, that'll cure them. But no I am sensitive enough to feel guilt, to think of helping. Is that what is meant by the cosiness of middle-class guilt – it makes you feel good? Yet they are so far gone and effective drying out or rehabilitation is so distantly remote that to achieve it would require my full-time attention for each person. Why can I not stand there and command the evil spirits to 'be silent and come out', leaving behind docile, reformed characters who give praise to God. They know my failure all right and they know how to twist the knife in my conscience: this is God's house, eh Father, and Jesus welcomes us all. I've got the words of a first-century Palestinian madman on my brain: I know thee who thou art, the Holy One of God. We, both of us, play a game of bluff which I shall call 'I know thee who thou art'. No you don't, yes I do, no you don't.

Joey I liked, for the easiest of reasons – that he liked

me. He possessed the spirit of giving and honesty. His honesty was like a knowing wink, like a fluttering butterfly delighting the eye while it lays the eggs of the destructive caterpillars that will eat my cabbages. He doesn't say, here I am, honest Joe, let me have some money for a bottle, he spins a yarn like all the others about accommodation and paying me back on Friday, but it is a convention he knows I understand, shows it in his eyes, and turns his begging into art for my amusement. That is what he gives me – this entertainment – and it is himself he gives.

On days of comparative equilibrium he would sweep the leaves, or collect up rubbish in the churchyard, and neatly stow the litter in the bins, working well, aggressively loyal, belonging. This I could give to him, and unreservedly offered to him, even if I knew his earnings would be spent on whisky. There is a story told in these parts that C. S. Lewis was once walking across Magdalene Bridge with his college chaplain when a tramp asked Lewis for some money. Lewis obliged, and as they walked on the chaplain objected that the money would only be spent on drink. To which Lewis replied – well, I suppose that is how I should have spent it myself.

I scarcely knew Joey. Perhaps it was part of his generosity that he kept his distance; he had his life and I had mine. It was better that way. Yet he told me that he liked to sweep the leaves because he had had a garden once, not very big, but his own, and he was glad that I knew about leeks and raspberries too. To look into his dirt-encrusted face, prematurely aged by alcohol poisoning and regret, required the patience of an archaeologist, who slowly, gently picks off the ancient mud and rock until he reveals the fossilised remains and is able to reconstruct a picture of what life might once have been like. Humour crouched there, a certain ironic humour, under tousled grey hair that still possessed a tint of redness, and pale freckled skin, blotched with roseate patches. At eighteen he had married a girl from his Glasgow street. He worked as a labourer and they lived with her mum until the bairn came along. Then they rented a ground-floor flat, with a bit of a garden. But work became scarce at home and he had to travel further and further south for jobs on big new building developments, until he became no more than a distant relative who paid the bills.

He still has the letter his wife sent when she left him. Each character, laboriously drawn, is as jagged as the message it contains.

Joey grew depressed. With money in his pocket, for six months he drank each night and through each weekend until the work ran out. Then he was free to drink each day as well, but with no income he had soon spent the rent money and had to sleep out rough. So he had spiralled down like a winged seed and taken root in the undergrowth of dossers and down-and-outs, druggies and piss-artists, kipping in hostels and churchyards, waiting down the social security, tapping passers-by for twenty pence.

We are all shaped by our pasts. Pasts which are infinitely meaningful to us, and almost as infinitely insignificant to others. Our pasts shout at us, unheard by the outside world, but inescapable to ourselves, like an inflammation of the vertebrae screwing up the nerves with silent and invisible pain. What do we know of each other's past? What can we know? What complex emotions were stored up at our mother's knee, or haunting sensitivities grew from our failures and rejections, just waiting beneath the surface until a new vulnerability releases them to taunt us? What do we know of each other's pasts: case notes in the doctor's, employer's, social worker's files or, if we are lucky, a curriculum vitae in a professional directory. We are like skulls, empty to each other. That skull had a tongue in it and could sing once. That bone had sinews and could run once. Once upon a time Joey was a father, but what had happened to the child who sat astride his shoulders laughing? And where was the woman who, aroused, had drawn his body close to hers? Yes, he had a past, and how he grieved for it, and raged with anger for it, and cursed his God for it.

The crucifix was made of ivory, the tooth-bone of the beleaguered and afflicted elephant, God's gentle-giant creature who was innocent enough to imagine that he could protect himself from predators by growing two shafts of beautiful bone out of his skull. And what happened? Men with pits and ropes, with spears and elephant guns, wasted his monumental flesh to wrench out those pitiful tusks. In their lust for money they slaughtered whole herds and families until in parts of Africa only stray individual beasts remain, neurotic and disoriented, searching hopelessly for their lost elephant society. The dreadful cost of that material probably never occurred to the sculptor, or maybe he considered it peculiarly appropriate to his subject. Painstakingly he had carved the agony of Christ in the misery of the elephant, using specific evidence of man's greed to illustrate the universality of his sin; one artist realising his vision of the divine artist, which now lay, as once it had in the arms of Joseph of Arimathea, broken.

There was Joey, as I say, before the forest of candles and Our Lady, serene and holy, with Christ's body broken for him, by him, on the altar. If we were to claim on the insurance then the police would have to be informed. But would we wish another elephant slaughtered? For God's sake just let it be. Relax. Cut the red tape. Forget responsibility for this inanimate shrine, glorious perpendicular, reverberant in history, resonant in too easily summarised pasts, this grade-one listed building, and behold the man. For here you see a bright, but impermanent miracle; Joey has heard and believed the voice that commanded, 'Be silent, and come out of him.'

*

In 1988 the local Council of Churches made a survey of the social concerns that each of them was engaged in, and an assessment of unmet social needs. The unanimous voice indicated that church communities felt impotent in the face of the challenge of homelessness. The report stated: 'There are a great many single homeless destitute people on the streets of our city, and their need seems to represent a reproach to Christians in an affluent society'. A reproach? How can Christians proclaim the gospel of Christ with integrity when they fail to attend to the very people whom Christ made a priority in his own ministry?

The first, and most revealing, step was to find out what the existing agencies for the homeless were already doing, and to be humbled by the discovery of the breadth of their commitment, expertise, and resourcefulness. How arrogant we had been to suppose that little was being done and that we Christians could step into the breach. In fact there was a view amongst the agencies that the churches were unable to get their act together on matters of social concern because ten years earlier they had provided accommodation for a night hostel which they were now wanting to take back for parish purposes.

The professionals mixed realism with compassion in a way that was both liberating and shocking to many of us. Street alcoholics were notoriously manipulative and ought not to be given money. Such payouts were naive, sentimental, dismissive and immoral. It was an easy way of ignoring another person's real needs and colluding with their self-destruction and their anti-social behaviour. Even to pay for 'a bed for the night' was to release funds for alcohol.

Twenty pence for a cup of tea was just as bad because tea was provided free at the day centre, where a person could sit and be warm, and unless he had persistently broken the rules, he would always be found overnight accommodation in one of the shelters.

However, there was one gap in the existing provisions – nowhere for people to go between four in the afternoon and seven in the evening, because that was the time when day staff were preparing to finish work and go home, and the period when the night shelter had to be cleaned. In summer this was not such a significant problem, but in the winter being forced to spend three hours in the cold every day is hard. The churches accepted the challenge.

# Joseph

'Husband, in faith, and that a-cold!
Ah, welaway, Joseph, as thou art old.'

'All old men, example take by me –
How I am beguiled here you may see –
To wed so young a child.'
(*The Annunciation*, Coventry Pageant)

Yes, Joseph knows his place; it is at the back of the crib,
where he stands dressed in a tunic of red, yellow, green and
blue stripes, over which he wears a rough camel-brown coat,
with headgear tied on by a bright red band around his
forehead. Actually, it is hard to distinguish him from the
shepherds. Which one is Joseph, the children ask when we
are taking the figures out the dust-encrusted box from the
church cellar. I identify him as the one whose bewilderment
is most poignantly captured in papier mâché, torn between
destiny and the bitter emotions of an ill-used husband. So
we place him there beside Mary, a dramatic convention, but
one who was not really in on the act.

He simply couldn't get it out of his mind. He must have
been over the events a million times: the disbelief when Mary
admitted she was pregnant, the anger, his desire to hit her,
to hurt her in some way, to leave here there and then and
let her cope as best she could. You are too old for her, his
family had said. A young girl like that needs to have a good
time. It won't last. Joseph listened, but ignored them,
because day by day she had come to his shop, and sat there
as he worked, animated, youthful, telling him her hopes and
ambitions, and looking to him as one with a bit of experience
for encouragement and advice. At first it seemed she saw
him as a father, but there was a physical vibrancy about
her that surprised him; and very slowly, for he was a shy
man, he began to recognise that her uninhibited, innocently

17

generous personality, expressed in confidence and touch, was meant for him in a special way. What a heady delight that realisation had been. Her kisses came as a gift beyond all hoping.

It was never quite the same afterwards, because however much he told himself that the angel in his dream was right, that the child was of God, he always had his doubts, jealous of someone, jealous of God, jealous of whoever took from him the maidenliness of his workshop girl, and caused her and her body to bear the marks of motherhood before he did, he the betrothed, the rightful husband, waiting honourably for the consummation of their marriage. Was he right to think that the eyes of those he met in the market place questioned his manhood, taunting him – husband, in faith, but a foolish one.

If he was reticent about his feelings, bottled them up, reluctance grew from the patience taught him by his being a craftsman. At work he was practised in self-forgetting; the adze, the chisel, the mallet, the saw, absorbed his ego like a poultice mollifies an ulcer, and all his creative aggression seemed to be channelled into the yoke or the salt box on his bench that he was making for a local farmer or householder. It was a kind of prayer, contemplation, in which the mind is emptied of all its self-regarding debris in the act of concentration. *Pure unpretentious very simple art is the best companion for the religious man.* Those who knew him loved him, described him as calm, good-humoured, even-tempered. And he was all the more attractive because he wore his religion like his easy-fitting tunic, natural and unostentatious, but not without colour – the finest style for a godly man. They said he was the last person who deserved to be beguiled.

Back in Nazareth amongst the homely date palms, pomegranates, and vineyards of that gentle land, he used to watch the child asleep in his cradle and wonder, wonder what he would have been like had he been his own. Brown eyes, perhaps, the mouth more slender and less inclined to bawl with such determination before his feed, or suddenly, inexplicably in the night. Who knows? Joseph regretted that the perfectly complexioned infant with translucent, veined eyelids sleeping there was not bone of his bone and flesh of his flesh. He could not permit himself the extravagance of that narcissistic love that sees oneself miraculously recreated in another, yourself refined, with all the potential for fulfilling your own fading ambitions – a child prodigy in the making, a future leader, to be respected, honoured, to make history.

The months in Bethlehem and Egypt had been cruel. First the bitter cold nights of the Judaean hills, then the rumour, no more than a scare, that paranoid Herod, fearing a palace coup, had ordered the execution of male infants under the age of two. There was a panic amongst the women. It seemed absurd, but to a tyrant who had had his own brother-in-law drowned in the River Jordan, and who burned, tortured and beheaded at will, any outrage was possible. So the exhausting, life-dangerous journey had been undertaken. Why bother? It was a chance in a thousand. Why not take a risk and head straight for home? He had proposed this, half thinking that enough had been required of him already. Her body sapped by childbirth and road-weary, out of her mental fatigue, Mary concurred. Until together they reflected that having followed the wild, irrational direction of God so far, it would be silly to let their commitment slip. Fear besieged the whole portentous journey, like an invitation into fatherhood. By day they walked and by night he kept watch over Mary and her little Moses, with the aid of a fire against the predatory wild beasts that might get the scent of milky flesh. When Mary became ill with a fever, he had to lodge her in an inn, find a wet-nurse for the child, and go each morning to the village market place hoping to be hired for casual work in order to pay the bill. Cleaning out the cattle sheds or clearing stones from the miserly fields, he spent his days praying she would not die, his darling carefree Nazareth girl with whom he had not even yet made love, much as he had desired her, leaving him with a child he did not ask for, like a curse upon his forbearance. Hunger ground his stomach like a granite mill-stone turned by the effort of his own muscles, as if he must himself squeeze and press the fever from her pallid skin. This he did not resent for the love he had for her. There was an intimacy between them created by her weakness, and the way it demanded his sacrifice of himself. She might have borne this child without him, but now his own gut-rending labour was indispensable, betrothal turned to marriage. In some way the birth was his too. So that as he unwrapped the soiled cloth and washed the baby, and became familiar with every detail of his perfect body, and caught, as he looked up between the waving toe-clenched feet, that bright-eyed, gummy smile which seemed to say, you are mine, he dreamt for a moment that once more he was at his bench lost in his simple uncomplicated art.

In the spring of the following year Joseph had become less anxious about his life. Past austerity has a way of focusing the present, making one super-sensitive to the ordinary and predictable, living each day as if it were an unexpected gift, so that the return to work seemed to him throughout that period no less than a holiday. He ate his food and drank his wine, savouring each mouthful with the astonished relish of a prisoner newly released from a diet of bread and water. Even the procreation-heralding birdsong possessed the unfathomable quality of musical genius. And the flowers spread across the hillside translucent and elated. With the child on his shoulders, they walked in the fields one sabbath day; Mary strode alongside them, face tilted up towards their faces, scrutinising each in turn, unpossessive. Fleetingly free of maternal responsibility, she stooped to pick flowers, daisies and harebells, and presented them to the outstretched hand of her child. Look, she said. Look how beautiful they are. You see, said Joseph, they cannot toil or spin, but not even King Solomon in all his splendour was dressed like one of these. Then they sat down on the green grass by a clump of trees, gazing contented over the flat roofs and limed walls of their village, while the child expertly manoeuvred his body towards the trees, running on all fours. Standing was his latest obsession, levering himself up against the bench, or holding his parents' fingers and walking recklessly away from the vertical. Now supporting himself with both hands against a tree, he turned his baby-rubber frame towards Joseph and smiled his broad-mouthed grin. Was he mocking or accepting? Perhaps in the laughter of all our children there is mockery and reliance. Then he took his first independent steps, four, five, six, seven, and fell into Joseph's lap, triumphant.

After the celebrations (being held aloft, extravagantly praised by both parents, trying again, succeeding) Mary, jubilant and grateful, announced to Joseph, what he had suspected but dared not hope, that she was pregnant, and by her calculations three months gone.

# Joseph

That is one way of telling the story – the version of orthodox theology, supported by Matthew and Luke, by the medieval miracle plays, fixed in our minds by Christmas carols, and the tradition of the Church. Indeed, not to tell it that way can be seen as disruptive and hostile to the Faith. But is there another version not incongruous with New Testament witness? Mark, Paul and John have no need for the virgin birth in putting their case for the incarnation. (No, you are quite wrong. I do not want a punch-up about the virgin birth. I am interested in the psychology of Joseph, because his relationship with Jesus must have been very formative.)

In his opening chapter John describes how Philip accepts immediately Jesus' call to discipleship and then, in his enthusiasm, finds Nathanael and says to him, 'We have found him of whom Moses in the law and also the prophets wrote, Jesus of Nazareth, the son of Joseph'.

The son of Joseph. Oh, no, that cannot be the case, say the commentators. This is the talk of disbelieving Jews who want to discredit the belief that Jesus came down from heaven. But in the same breath Philip had just claimed that Jesus was the Messiah, foretold by the prophets. How can that be thought disbelieving? To which the commentators reply: well, yes, but in his prologue John tells us that all who believed in the name of Jesus were given power to become children of God, who were then 'born not of the will of the flesh, nor of the will of man, but of God'. Oh, I see. So you are suggesting that because Jesus is the Son of God, therefore he was born not of the will of the flesh, but of God. Exactly.

That seems rather like fixing your experiments to produce the results you have decided you want. Besides, two chapters later Jesus tells Nicodemus that entry to the Kingdom of God requires both physical birth and a metaphorical spiritual rebirth, the rebirth of faith, of heavenly values. So that which comes down from heaven can be incarnated in the natural way, and then be spiritually born again. Do the divine genes necessarily have to be imparted by the 'shadowing' of the Holy Spirit? Do we not believe that we are able to share in Christ's divinity by the even greater miracle of God's transforming grace?

The son of Joseph. So the child was his all along. When the first waves of attraction stirred the air between the carpenter and his pupil of the philosophy of life, it was with a sense of chaste delight. And not only betrothal, but discreet and creative consummation followed joyfully. It did not seem out of place, irresponsible, but reverent and celebratory. Indeed, it was not inappropriate that the child who when a man was to cure on the sabbath day, and send the hypocrites running, running, running, teasing them for tithing even their dried herbs while neglecting the fundamental laws of love for God and neighbour, should in his conception observe the spirit, if not the letter, of the law. God comes in humility, born to poverty, born an outsider, conceived a bastard. Only the lowest, most emptied God can exalt the lowly and weak. Only our dishonesty about sexuality, the childish fear that sex is dirty, the silent conspiracy that sex tarnishes religion, causes us to flinch and allow the charge of blasphemy to stick.

Yes, his eyes were blue, deep blue, not brown, and penetrated Joseph's own admiring fatherly gaze, as if they could see into his soul, not judging or accusing, but adoring, wanting to be at one. Like any other dad Joseph played the who-does-he-take-after game. He's got your hands, dear. And something of his grandfather's chin. But genetic attributions are ambiguous, equivocal, given the miraculous uniqueness of each combination. Certainly the broad mouth, generous in laughter and demanding on the ear, was not a family characteristic. Joseph thought it oddly and strangely different. Yet here was no infant prodigy, no myth too great for babyhood. He was struggling to incarnate his thoughts and feelings into words of Aramaic.

# Moving House

Outside the shrine in the piazza a wheelchaired girl of eight or nine, shouting with laughter, is trying to lever herself up by her arms into a standing position. Excited parents and friends, gathered round her, one holding the handles of the chair, exchange hopeful chatter, like gossip. Look, she wants to stand. Praise the Lord. Does that new twitch mean that some dormant muscle has been freed? Miracles do happen. Wouldn't it be wonderful.

Among the group, attended by nuns in nursing habit, are other sick and handicapped children, other wheelchairs, a boy on crutches, a girl who can't see. They arrived by bus with a British number plate. You watched the children being lowered on its hydraulic lift and guessed this was a pilgrimage of healing, sponsored perhaps by a local church, which had raised the money by raffles, bazaars and sponsored walks. How appealing it would have been to walk for those who cannot walk. The piazza buzzed with expectancy and bewilderment, like a great hospital concourse where some waited nervously to go in and others emerged from the inner sanctum rejoicing, drained, hyped-up, mystified, unready to slide back into their lives just yet. All had given themselves up with trusting or nothing-to-lose passivity, placing their destiny in the hands of another. Now pulses raced in anticipation of what manner of judgement this day would bring. What has happened to me? Has anything happened to me? Please, let something happen to me? While the carers, the nuns, priests, nurses and pilgrimage organisers conduct themselves with quiet beatific confidence. They know the psychosomatic power of assurance, they are not shy of extravagant hope. The ability of God to make his children whole through sacred objects, holy stones or the Black Madonna's eyes, does not embarrass them. Why should it?

Their art is to think positive and to pray positive. They do not pretend to understand the ways of God.

You approach the child, the girl you first noticed, seeking with your eyes the permission of those you assume to be her parents. You speak to her, and she seems relieved that someone neutral, probably even indifferent to her condition, at least emotionally outside it, is willing to break the tension that the accumulation of expectancy, built up over the months of fund-raising and the religious chorus-singing on the bus journey across Europe, has created. You get chatting about Northampton, where she comes from, and the convent school she attends, about faith and the fact that you are not a Catholic, and possibly no longer a Christian. Then she asks, with an air of genuine intellectual enquiry, 'How did Mary's House come to Loreto?'

## II

'When the guardian angels of the holy house at Nazareth saw that it was about to be destroyed by men of another religion, they thought they heard the stones cry out "Preserve us. For we are those who heard our Saviour's speech and kept guard over him during his sleep. We are blessed and with this blessing have the power to heal." Then the angels said to one another, "Is not our God the God of the air as well as the God of the land and sea? Let us therefore lift these sacred stones and fly them to a Christian land where people will honour them and receive their blessing." So in the year 1291, with whirring wings and a mighty thrust of air, the four angels lifted the house into the stratosphere, in an aurora of light, and transported it towards Italy. Across Cyprus they came, across the Cyclades, the mainland of Greece, into Yugoslavia, and as they reached the Dalmatian coast their wings had grown so tired bearing their heavy load that they came down to rest. Three years later, which was the time it took for their energy to be restored, with one final effort, they flew the house once more into the cold, thin air and placed it in Loreto, here on this great hill, looking out over the blue water of the Adriatic and the domed summit of Monte Conero. This, by the way, is how the Madonna of Loreto won the name of Protectress of Aviators.'

'Aviators', said the little girl. 'What are they?'

'Pilots. People who fly.'

'One day I shall be an aviator. One day I shall fly and pray for the boys and girls below who can only walk and run.' Breathless, she paused, then looked up into your face with such an expression of help-my-unbelief that you wanted to gouge out your very self, if it could be of any use, and give it to her. 'Shall I ever fly?' she asked. 'Yes, you shall fly. You must fly.' Then you said, part to her parents, part to her. 'Wait here. Don't go away. I'll be back.'

## III

You had approached the shrine reluctantly, having laughed at its story over a glass of wine the previous night in a conversation where liberal rationalism won hands down, as you never doubted it would, nor wished otherwise. You were afraid that the human race would embarrass you with its superstition and credulity or that you would be angered by the exploitation of commercial and spiritual mountebanks trying to rip you off. But as soon as you drove over the ridge and saw the distant basilica, sharp and focused in the clear light, like an arrangement of elaborate terracotta urns in a beautiful renaissance garden, crowned by an immense silver dome, you drove eagerly on. From the seaside resorts, seven or eight kilometres away, it must have seemed alluring and magical.

In the city the spiral street that climbs to the piazza outside the church led you bumper to bumper in a procession with other day trippers through a gorge of burnt-sienna houses, opening into a wide street-bazaar. You ran the gauntlet of pedlars selling gaudy souvenirs, religious and secular side by side, without discrimination. Featureless cheap ceramic madonnas mingle with luminous pink, green and red soft toys that blink, jump and squeak. Silver balls on a rotating arm catch rays of light in blinding reflections that contrive to make the sun seem vulgar. From the striped awnings dangle all sizes and colours of rosary beads, crosses, crucifixes, chains, necklaces, brooches and charms, and on the white walls of the shops behind the trinket-laden stalls, are plaques, and plates, and tiles all depicting a house flying through the air. In the crush of tourists browsing, sticky tempers begin to tease like questions in a moral philosophy paper. Children insist on the most expensive ice-creams only to smear the great bronze figure of Pope John XXIII with amareno and pistacchio, while he continues to smile forgivingly, stretching out bright fingers, licked to a shine by pilgrims' kisses.

No doubt just as the road to hell is paved with good intentions so the approach to the pearly gates will be lined with hucksters in baseball caps flogging souvenirs. You ask yourself what this tawdry show has to do with human beings celebrating something holy, trying to excavate their deep responses, wanting to articulate their most lofty hopes and aspirations. What draws people here? Is it a search for meaning and value amidst two weeks of self-indulgence in the sun and sea? Is it the architecture of Giuliano da Maiano, Baccio Pontelli, Francesco di Giorgio Martini, and Donato Bramante? Or the paintings of Luca Signorelli, Melozzo da Forlì and Lorenzo Lotto? Or the fact that it is said that beneath that great dome lie stones touched by Jesus Christ himself? You were confused by this speculation and wished that the shrine bore the same clarity and focus close to that you had observed from a distance.

Your guidebook offered an exegesis, a demythologising which ought to be helpful to your sceptical mind. Archaeological investigations carried out beneath the holy house in the 1960s established that the stones of Mary's house were indeed carried from Nazareth to Dalmatia in the thirteenth century, and thence to Loreto, but not by angels. Instead, it was a group of Christians who took them there by ship. It goes on to offer a theological critique: 'What in fact really matters to the faithful is not the miraculous angelic flight, but the poignant religious significance of the house of the Madonna where Jesus lived to his thirtieth year; a house which evokes the mystery of the Incarnation and the daily life of the Holy Family'. But you ask yourself what use are explanations. Do explanations really ever reveal the meaning of miracles? For example, when Jesus walked on the water does the idea that he might have come out on stepping-stones just beneath the surface actually serve to confirm your faith? No, these reductions diminish it.

So a fragment of the Holy Land has been reconstructed in the Italian Marches with stones rendered holy by the proximity which they once bore to Jesus Christ and his family, in an attempt to define, and locate, and explain, and illustrate, and capture, and possess the elusive, all-engulfing infinity of the power of God. It is no more than Jesus memorabilia, not unlike Elvis or Beatles memorabilia, trying to cork the genie in the bottle, to distil the spirit of the man, and the events which surrounded him in a tangible, graspable form. Didn't he give a warning to those who wished to follow him: 'Foxes have holes and birds of the air have nests, but the Son of Man has nowhere to lay his head'? Wasn't there something about him rejecting home, and family ties, and a steady income, and a promising future, because in order to demonstrate the true nature of God he had to sacrifice material security with all its strings attached which tie you down to this moral compromise or that physical affection, and open himself completely to God's will? That had always appealed to you. You recognised the virtue of his integrity, but had rejected the organisation that had appointed itself to safeguard his message, not primarily because of the organisation's own hypocrisy, but because of its unconvincing soppiness. They asserted that he was perfect God and perfect man, and therefore blandly assumed that his home life must necessarily have conformed to a women's-magazine pastiche of the ideal happy family. Even if his heredity was impeccable, and you didn't wish to debate this, what about his environment? Which shapes a personality more, heredity or environment? Was his a life without arguments, sulking, or temper tantrums, or fighting with brothers, always going to bed when you are told, and helping with the washing up? What a wonderful relationship they must have had, and how these stones evoke its poignancy. Doesn't it make you envious, guilty? Well does it? Don't we all know that relationships only grow and develop through experiencing and overcoming tension and disagreement, trial and error, mistakes and failure? And that although it is painful and difficult, parents have first to say no to their children, and later be ready to set their children free to be themselves? All these commonplace tensions of family life must have been witnessed by the holy stones of Loreto. If only they could speak. Jesus cast away his home and his family when he went to Galilee. He had, to put it in his own strong words, left the dead to bury their own dead.

## IV

You were not convinced. You saw many hands not waving, but drowning. A forest of hands in the sea of doubt and insecurity, your own among them. If only we had the wings of faith to rise above the water into the bright air, you thought. And you ran back to the shops where you searched for the plate which seemed to you to depict the flying house in the most artistic manner. When you presented it to the handicapped girl it was wrapped in pink tissue paper. She unwrapped it with all the speed her undexterous hands could manage, and when she saw the house she gave out a throaty scream of pleasure, which made others on the piazza turn quickly thinking she was in distress. You kissed her. The parents clucked and looked on, touched, amazed by all the willing that their daughter should be whole, even though lack of oxygen at birth was the explanation. But what use are explanations?

You whispered to her, 'One day you shall fly. You must fly.' She passed the plate to you to hold, and with an effort of every available muscle taut and strained within her body, she brought herself to a standing position and reached out her arms, like wings, to the crowd that had now gathered round.

# Excuses, Excuses

There were those who excused *themselves* because of Meredith, people of the there-but-for-the-grace-of-God-go-I school. Then there was Meredith and his endless self-justification. And, of course, there were those to whom his excuses meant nothing, only made it worse. And, most surprising of all, there was the curious way those who were so nearly hurt by him, forgave him, as if they understood something that everyone else had failed to see.

So this could be a story about sin and forgiveness, except that people don't sin any more, they simply act anti-socially or inconsiderately, compelled by circumstances of environment or upbringing into behaviour for which other people (society, their parents) must take the blame.

Meredith never believed he would end up in prison, perhaps for that reason; that although he could see some might consider his behaviour socially unacceptable, it was not deeply wrong, not inexcusably wrong, it possessed its own Freudian explanation. He honestly never thought it would come to this, because he was convinced that what he had done was nothing other than the expression of genuine affection, and the boy, who the judge repeatedly reminded us was only eleven years old, had gladly consented.

Three weeks later I was permitted to visit him. I had never been in a prison before, only in a Borstal, which wasn't quite the same. As I drove over the rooftops of Paddington, through its steeples and crumbling stucco facades, I began to experience the guilty excitement of morbid fascination for what I was about to see. Not even shame could fight it off. I knew I was about to gawp, just as the public gawps at the explicit newspaper pictures of other people's suffering in the aftermath of a tragedy.

The chaplain led me first through a Victorian block in which the iron staircases climbed like fire escapes in a geometric abstract painting. Cast your eyes one way and the steps are ascending, cast them another and they are descending, but however you look they seem to have no beginning and no end. And if you could add music to this impression, it would be the tympanic off beat rhythm of jangling keys, closing doors, and the clank of the men's boots on the metal stairs. Above our heads stretched the safety nets, like giant hammocks, ready to catch any prisoner who should attempt to escape by jumping from the upper landings. It was impossible not to think of the circus and the trapeze artist stepping out with tentative balletic steps across the high wire, long pole flapping like a great prehistoric bird, and glittering, shapely, body-stockinged girls spinning in a whirl of limelight on a rope clenched between their teeth. With what freedom they had flown through the cavernous spaces of the big top. With what grace they had trampolined from the net to the sawdust, amidst the clapping and cheering, to arch their bodies in joyful recognition of the crowd.

'I must show you the chapel before we go up', said the chaplain. 'Splendid Victorian Gothic. Built to enshrine the triumph of good over evil.' We went inside. It was true, the building rose in lofty, aspiring redbrick grandeur.

'Where are the safety nets?' I asked.

He explained with pleasure that the services were well attended. At least here the mind could be adjusted, oriented, re-tuned by some reference to human history and creative achievement, even if it were the product of high Victorian self-confidence. When art is in short supply one savours it and relishes it as a starving man eats a scrap of bread.

Meredith had been attending the daily eucharist, and would like to become a server. No, you must pronounce his name 'M'Reddith', Meredith Williams. He is most particular about that. It is his Welshness, you see. And although he has lived in London for the fifteen years of his adult life, his heart is in the Rhondda where his mother lives, and where his father died in a pit accident in 1962. It has surprised many of us how this shy, gentle, warmhearted man has conducted such a determined campaign to hear his name pronounced correctly, even on one occasion correcting the Borough Youth Officer in public. But it shouldn't surprise us. I remember how he was when I threatened to close the youth club after the Tasker gang had broken into the hall and smashed up all the tables, and left their nasty graffiti on the walls. In my study he refused to take a seat, but stood there with the electric light reflecting on his head through his thinning, downy hair, and his bulgy eyes popping more than usual, silent. I had no reason not to trust him. He did a good job. Now he was imploring me with this hang-dog look and quivering lip. 'But I love these children', was all he said. Then at last he sat down, and I went and made him a cup of tea.

Of course he loved the children, I knew that. Anyone could see they were his life. Immersed in his speech therapy during the day (Come on now, you can do it for Meredith) and running the youth club at nights. I never doubted that his kindness, his attention, his arm round the shoulder, grew out of his immense capacity for love. I sometimes worried, though, I admit, that he cared too much, and occasionally heard spiteful comments. The children called him 'Ever Reddy', and I was never sure whether this contained a *double entendre*, or was, which was more likely, a feeble pun on his name and electric batteries. But my job is to nurture and encourage love, the source and the pinnacle of Christian virtue – Brethren let us love one another, for love is of God – not to stifle the love of those who are good at it, just because I have a suspicious mind. Love is a risky business. Who truly succeeds at it?

We approached the cell block on the third floor. More keys. Doors closing behind. Here the chaplain left me. I was relieved that two men in their denim-blue prison suits were playing ping-pong. Somehow the click, ti, click, ti, click, of ball on bat and table, eased the tension. Meredith must enjoy the familiarity of that sound too.

He was waiting in a side room, at a formica-topped table. When he stood up we shook hands, and he looked at me in that way of his. He looked at me as if he loved me, as if he were waiting for words of salvation, or words like, wake up, it is only a dream. When I put the three Mars bars and the Coke on the table he saw something to laugh at, and we were both grateful. Prisoners were not permitted to keep gifts of food and drink, but during an interview they were allowed to consume what they could.

We sat down either side of the table. He shifted nervously on his hams, I think because of the prison officer in the corner who was there to supervise our interview, but who in fact concentrated on picking his nails, bored. Meredith beckoned me to lean closer, as if he still might have secrets. I asked him how he was. He was cross. He wanted to appeal. The judge had misunderstood.

'You have always misunderstood me', he said, contemplating his hands folded upon the table. 'I know what you think of me. You would never say it, at least not in so many words, but you think I'm a pervert – like the rest of them here.' I decided not to protest, but let him continue. 'Peter was my friend, a real friend. It is possible for an older man to be friends with a child, you know. There is something rather beautiful about it, really. It just went a bit too far. We loved each other, and it went a bit too far. Peter was quite happy about it – he didn't mind. It was all so natural. If it hadn't been for Peter telling Tommy, and Tommy telling his mum, none of this would have happened. It was all Tommy's fault.'

'You are a silly fool', I said. 'You can't go on making excuses. It won't do you any good. If you want God's forgiveness, he will forgive you, but only when he knows you take your sin seriously. Look, children make unreliable judgements. They haven't enough experience to do otherwise. But adults are expected – well, they are expected to be grown up, responsible, capable of discernment, at least to act within the law. You were entrusted by society with the care of children, and although apparently you do not think so, you have abused that trust, and look what society has done with your excuses . . .'

What had society done with his excuses? Locked them up in a place where he could not go to the lavatory in private, or use one at all at night. Locked them up in a cell with two other men, one of whom persistently forced his sexual attentions, which, despite what you might think, was obnoxious to Meredith. It had wrapped them in boredom and hopelessness, and locked them in that cell often for twenty-three hours out of twenty-four, and hoped that they would be swilled down the drains at slopping-out time.

Mind you, society offers its own excuses in return. Overcrowding, the rising crime rate, increased custodial sentences. What do you expect? We are not running holiday camps.

One of the important functions of imprisonment is that it should be a deterrent.

Clearly Meredith didn't like what I had said, considered it unsympathetic, perhaps unchristian. I would have to try to convince him later that God values us all, whom he has made in his own image, but that part of his valuing of us is to expect the best from us. Acceptance and expectation go hand in hand. Somehow, God knows how, I must proclaim release to the captives.

So he sulked for a while and we both gazed out of the window, across the wall and the electrified fencing to the rooftops beyond. He put the can to his mouth and took a swig of Coke, which fizzed up into his nose causing him to splutter, pathetically, over the table.

How does the world outside look to him on this watery, dull November afternoon, I wondered. Close, yet distant, the early lights of London begin to sparkle like stars, beckoning, yet inaccessible. Did he ever walk free, as I was soon to do? Did he ever walk free? When did the gradual realisation come upon him that love was so difficult. First that he could not love women, then that he could not love men? Or that they would not love him? But that in childish relationships there was the hope of fulfilment? Like those few happy years before puberty in the junior school, before they started to taunt him about his popping eyes, and soft, gentle voice (a kind melodious voice, lilting like the green valleys) before the monster, the devil on his back, had begun to grip him in a stranglehold, and take hold not only of his neck, but of other parts as well – parts that now, to escape his captivity, he would suffer to be gouged out like Oedipus' eyes. How will the world outside appear to him in six months, in a year? Or is there some immune mechanism that comes into play to freeze you against the outside?

In half an hour he will be back in his cell with his cell mates. He knows it. I am looking forward to half-past four, I admit, and the drive home. I love driving in London, even in the rush hour. So he turns to me again, fingering the purple bruise under his left eye. He knows that if I am heartless about his self-justification, the fact of personal suffering will certainly soften me up.

'What happened to your face?' I asked, trying to give that reassurance he needed.

'Oh, it was nothing.'

'It looks very uncomfortable.'

'It's nothing. Tell me about Jonathan, and Tony and Patricia. How have they taken it?'

He wanted to hear about friends at home and how they had reacted to reports of his trial in the local newspaper. Whether they were angry? Were they disgusted? Could he ever come back again?

Tony and Patricia were typical of many parents who sent their children to the youth club in that they had got to know Meredith, welcomed him into their homes, fed him, been pleased to see him taking a particular interest in their son. They hadn't recognised that in a sense they were looking after another child. Naturally there was anger, but there was also incredulity, not of the would-you-believe-it gossipy kind, but parents' incredulity at their own naivete. Now, perhaps because of their very gullibility, they were accepting. I had been astonished in the months between arrest and trial, when Meredith was still living in the community, at the compassion and maturity with which he was accepted by those whom he had most nearly hurt. Only Peter's parents, whom I never met, remained bitter towards him. Although he did see them a few times, and tried to talk them into seeing things his way. I had expected ostracism, and violence – at least violence of language, if not a beating-up in a dark alley. Even Harry, the bricklayer, who had once nearly knocked my head off for letting his son cross the road by himself after a confirmation class, took Meredith to the White Hart for a drink. As for scandal. Well, scandal is a cheap thrill, as quickly forgotten as it is enjoyed, and what we saw was the community's natural capacity, given time, to hate the sin but love the sinner.

'They are fine. They are thinking of you, and send you their love. They would like to write if you can tell me when you are allowed to receive a letter.'

I knew Meredith really wanted to tell me how he got that corker on his left cheek; I knew he wanted me to be able to give him the sympathy he could recognise as love and forgiveness. So I asked him again, 'Come on, Reddy, what did you do to your face?'

He pulled me into a close tête-à-tête, until I could smell the odour of his breath.

On arrival at the prison he had to decide whether he wished to be placed in the wing for protected prisoners, but had chosen not to. Of course he was nervous, but he preferred what he called the 'jungle' to accepting a self-image of untouchability, a social leper, or worse, as he put it himself, 'a screwed up pervert'. He really thought he could make it.

'So what did you say you were in for?' I asked.

'Manslaughter. Dangerous driving. Killing a cyclist when driving home blind drunk.'

Did that story really fit his personality? He was not insensitive to the problem, and had tried to be brazen, even callous, but they were not easily convinced. After a long cross-examination from one of the second-floor bullies he guessed they were beginning to rumble him. Or had one of the screws let it slip, accidentally on purpose, that he was a child molester? The prison officers, he thought, shared a law-of-the-jungle morality in which sex offenders deserved what was coming to them. Then a few mornings later he had been carrying his overnight slop bucket to the toilets, along with the other men, when someone accidentally tripped him. The mess went all over the floor, and as he instinctively bent down to deal with it, a head met him full in the face. It was all over in a moment. There was laughter. Someone shouted, 'I'd drive more carefully in future if I were you'.

He was berated by the authorities for his carelessness and made to clear up. The next day he requested to be moved to the special block. They had not accepted his excuses.

Sometimes in the face of anarchy and chaos we feel an impotence which turns a vicious circle in our minds. Repeatedly we give an explanation, only to discover that no one understands what we are talking about, like knocking on a door that isn't there, like climbing up the iron stairs which have no beginning and no end, only a safety net to prevent us taking the ultimate alternative route. That was the impotence which exuded from Meredith when the minute hand reached four-thirty and the officer, suddenly come to life, simply said 'OK. That's it, son'. The prisoner rose, left a fading smile, and followed like a dog that had learned the folly of disobedience.

Do you know what I did on the way home? I would

like to know what you would have done. I would like to
know how you would have proclaimed release to the captives.
Or do you take the view that such as Meredith never change?
They serve their time, are discharged, and then set up the
same scenario all over again? How would you pray for this
man, who is only a figment of my imagination?

Do you know what I did on the way home? On the way
home I made a speech. I am sitting in the car in a three-
lane traffic jam, being gawped at by other drivers, who seeing
me waving my hands about must think I'm off my trolley.
But I am feeling emotional, churned up. A big chunk of me
is still trying to get free from that frightening, oppressive
place, the part of me, I guess, that felt it ought to be there,
deserved to be there, might end up there yet.

Men and women everywhere, of all times and all places.
Fellow prisoners: prisoners of the mind, locked in fear and
delusion; prisoners of failure, of place and upbringing, pacing
around the closed rooms of your past; prisoners of the body,
strapped in a wheelchair, trapped by your body chemistry,
frightened by the decay of beauty; prisoners of arrogance,
stunned by success, by never-found friendship; prisoners of
conscience, tortured, sleepless; the shackled, the beaten, the
frozen, the starved, murderers, criminals, extortioners. Fellow
prisoners. Listen. Love can survive. Does survive. And breaks
forth from the tomb.

# Changing Faces

(Based on an idea by Peter Carey from a short story in *Exotic Pleasures*)

When the television van pulled up outside the church, Mr Carpenter stroked his moustache and thought, that should put an end to it. Had ever a woman been so taken for granted, so exploited, so used, as his wife had been by the congregation at St Mark's? How many times had he implored her not to allow them to take advantage of her good nature? How many times had he come home to an oven-dry dinner and a note on the kitchen table – gone to a meeting. Back later? But this should change everything.

Katharine Carpenter, who believed that the local Christian community, despite all its faults, still had the power to celebrate the love of God in the world, hated to see any job left undone, and never shared her husband's cynicism. Even after Mr Cox had written his bullying editorial in the magazine, naming no names of course, but deploring the interference of parish busybodies, she agreed to help him with his special features project. She must have taken photographs of nearly all of us and written a short biographical note to accompany each one, all because the vicar had asked Mr Cox to use the magazine to help parishioners to get to know each other better.

We felt sorry for poor old Arthur Cox, the newsagent, because everyone could see that behind his bluff facade and ruby-wine nose he was all in a tizzy and hadn't got a clue what to do. But to Mrs Carpenter it was plain sailing. You see she was a very practical sort of person. Just down the road from the church, in her four-bedroomed semi, with its wisteria growing up over the front porch, and wonderful summer display of delphiniums in the front garden, she had a studio which she and Mr Carpenter had built over the

37

garage. It was in this studio that she did her freelance model-making. Sometimes the V & A would phone her at short notice and say that they wanted a Victorian interior, or a Greek temple, or water-mill for their latest exhibition, and she would produce it with the uncanny knack of one who could replicate in tangible form what she saw in her mind's eye, without the use of a ruler. Mr Carpenter used to joke that she could have made her fortune as a forger, especially with those innocent blue eyes. Nor was she anybody's fool. Twenty-five years ago she had won a scholarship to Cambridge, but was too meticulous. Her history supervisor complained at having to read forty pages when ten would do, and after a year she gave up the intricacies of history and started making models instead.

In fact she made the figures for our Christmas crib, big figures, about four feet tall, out of papier mâché on a wire frame, with skilfully designed clothes in brilliant colours. Each face had the individual character and depth of an Old Master painting such as you see on a Christmas card, a Rembrandt or a Raphael. And just as the painters, it is said, used local people as their subjects, so some members of the congregation claimed that they were the inspiration behind the shepherds and the kings. Indeed, if you put a pair of broad-rimmed spectacles on Caspar, as had been done once for fun, he looked just like Mr Jackson the sacristan, who was immensely flattered. I think later he regretted having been so pleased about this.

However, there was one thing that Mrs Carpenter refused to do. She always turned down invitations to speak in public. For example, the Women's Guild if they had asked her once must have asked her a hundred times to give an illustrated lecture at their monthly meeting, but she always said no in that disarming way of hers. I am not sure whether this was because of the powdery shortbread biscuits, served with the tea beforehand, which impacted in and around your gums until you were scarcely able to utter, or because she found her lisping impediment of speech an embarrassment. If it was the latter then it was silly because none of us really noticed.

I remember one occasion when I was talking with the vicar after a service she came up and said to him, rather generously I thought, how much she had enjoyed his sermon.

'I don't know how you do it', she said, 'a new sermon every week.' If ever you said anything like that to him he would draw in his breath between his teeth causing a hissing sound, almost like a tea-taster tasting tea except without the slurp, slurp, slurp that follows, and raise his eyebrows in what I can only describe as humble pride. 'Oh, you could do just as well, Mrs Carpenter', he said. Then, after a pause, 'Better in fact, I'm sure'. At the time he was trying to arrange a series of sermons by lay people in which they would preach the sermon which each of us has in us. Katharine was very apologetic and said that no one would want to hear what she had to say, and in any case she was having to devote nearly all of her spare time to making the model she had promised for the St Mark's centenary exhibition.

My husband and I had got to know Mrs Carpenter when we went on the parish pilgrimage to the Holy Land. I had just taken early retirement from teaching after thirty years, and Janice our youngest had been married in the spring. Our other daughter, Elspeth, we hardly ever see. She is a policewoman up in Yorkshire and if she has a boyfriend she doesn't tell us about him.

When I walked out of the staff-room and down the steps of Park Street Primary School for the last time it was like walking out of my life. It had never crossed my mind in previous summers, but now I felt a deep sadness for my old classroom, with its walls stripped bare of the children's work, and choking with that fetid smell like the odour of plimsolls warmed by the sun through locked windows. I even used to make a detour when going to the shops to avoid driving down Park Street. It was when I owned up to that that Bill said we should get away for a holiday.

Our room was next to Mrs Carpenter's on the top floor of a hotel near the Damascus Gate. (Mr Carpenter had stayed at home, not because he had no interest in travel – quite the contrary in fact, but because, he said, he couldn't bear to have religion rammed down his throat when he was trying to enjoy himself.) From our window we looked out across the skyline of the Old City of Jerusalem, an array of fortifications, walls and towers, interspersed with the little white domes of houses bulging like mushrooms in a field of television aerials. The first time the three of us walked through the gate into the bazaar beneath this canopy I felt as if at any moment Ali Baba and the Forty Thieves might appear from nowhere, so I said to Bill that he had better look after my handbag. It greatly amused Katharine to see this Englishman clad in khaki shirt and shorts surrounded by spices, carpets, exotic fruits and radios blaring out Arab music, carrying a handbag.

At one corner, where the narrow street turned sharply back on itself, two boys with sticks were thrashing insanely at a horse across its flanks. The animal was harnessed by a rope to three large logs which had become snagged and the rope chafed against the acute angle of the turn. As the horse struggled to obey, his body strained and poured sweat, his hooves kept slipping backwards across the cobblestones so that he fell and scrambled back up into a standing position, and his nostrils flared out in desperation. All the time the boys yelled and lashed out without understanding. This was not what we had come to see. At least it was not what I expected to see. From that moment Jerusalem haunted me as a place of suffering. When I looked up at the street sign and saw that we were on the 'Via Dolorosa', my heart missed a beat.

Of course we were taken on many guided tours that week, and the vicar gave a number of devotional talks. (Lucky for Mr Carpenter that he stayed at home!) But Mrs Carpenter seemed to know more than any of them about the places we visited, having done her homework with a thoroughness that made me feel guilty that I was not taking it all seriously enough. 'The trouble is', she said, 'the Jerusalem that Jesus walked is twenty feet under the ground.' Then she explained how the cycle of destruction and rebuilding had over the centuries buried the streets and the pools and the gates he would have known. She was very anxious to discover any site or stone which was contemporary with Jesus, as if these were clues to his personality or his meaning, or possessed a precious numinous (her word) power. We made a point of revisiting any place that seemed genuine in this way, like the Pool of Bethesda where the halt and blind bathed for healing when the angel 'troubled the waters', and where Jesus cured the man who had been sick for thirty-eight years. Or the pathway that leads up the side of the Kidron Valley, opposite the Mount of Olives, to Caiaphas' house. I think we were all impressed to think that these were probably the steps along which Jesus was dragged by the soldiers after his arrest. And when we visited the Church of St Peter 'In Gallicantu', which, the guidebook says, means 'at the cockcrow', and went into the underground dungeon where Jesus might have spent his last night, an awesome silence fell over the whole party. The prison is a natural cave in the rock, gouged out by water, like the inside of a stone pitcher, the depth of four men. Imagine the isolation of any man lowered by a rope into this dark pit, feeling with his hands against the steep smooth walls like a spider trapped in a bath.

Mrs Carpenter often mentioned to me that in all these places she had a feeling that something was not quite right. 'There is something missing. There is something missing.' But she would never say what it was – if she knew.

I was expecting a model in a glass case, but when we arrived there were still small puddles in the toytown streets left by a recent shower. As a matter of fact the model of Jerusalem at the time of the Second Temple in the grounds of the Holyland Hotel wasn't on our itinerary, but Katharine had read about it, and found a bus, at a fraction of the cost of a taxi, that would take us through the high-rise buildings and smart suburban homes of modern Jerusalem, to the door. I wish Bill and I could take that kind of initiative. It's so easy to miss out otherwise. Katharine, of course, was in her seventh heaven, studying this model which must have been the size of her own back garden. Just look at the colonnades in the Temple. What detail. And the materials – real stone. There's the Fortress Antonia, and down here is the Pool of Siloam. You can see how the boundaries of the city have changed since the time of Christ, so that Calvary is now inside the city wall. This is superb, absolutely superb. Yet, even so, I can't help feeling there is something missing.

After each day's sightseeing we caught the bus up to the Holyland Hotel where we took a drink in the modern lounge before going outside to refer to the model, mapping out in our minds what we had seen, and relating it to how things were in the first century. Bill, who had spent most of his life working in town planning, began to find this tiresome, so he tended to stay in the bar and drink arak, a sort of pernod-type drink that you add water to, which for him was one of the major revelations of the holiday. No, that's not fair. But he did enjoy it. The vicar, who I tried to persuade not to wear his dog-collar all the time in such humid weather, grew curious about our early evening expeditions, so on the Thursday we took him with us, and Katharine gave him her guided tour, which had by this time developed more into a seminar. 'Most fascinating. Most fascinating', he said afterwards. 'Perhaps you might change your mind and preach a sermon about this. Why don't you? It would be so good to have a *woman* take part in the series.'

If anything the Bishop was, in the opinion of most of us, overdressed for the opening of the centenary exhibition, especially as it wasn't a service. But I suppose he felt he needed his cope and pointed hat to do justice to the occasion. Ten rows of pews had been removed from the back of the church to make way for the various exhibits: old photographs, arts and crafts, the history of the choir, and so on. But in the centre, on a raised platform, hidden under an enormous suspended dust cover, ironically nicknamed 'the veil of the Temple', was Mrs Carpenter's contribution. At the appropriate moment the dust cover, which really looked like a great marquee, would be raised by the pulley that Mr Carpenter had fixed to the beam above. First the Bishop was to say a prayer of dedication, which was full of embroidered phrases to match his cope – the cope made for Bishop Fuller in 1886, the year St Mark's was built (of course, that explains it) – phrases like 'we do praise thee', and 'that thou wouldest bless', and 'the fruits of our handiwork'. Then he waved his hand in the air in what everyone except for Mr Carpenter understood to be a blessing. Mr Carpenter began to tug at the rope like Tarzan climbing into the trees and the veil of the temple flapped into the air, cutting the bishop short. Immediately the model was revealed, a gasp of appreciation filled the church, followed by spontaneous applause.

What we saw before us was a composite of scenes from the gospels beautifully juxtaposed in a stunning tableau: a part of the Temple, colonnaded, a Jerusalem street, the interior of a banqueting hall, and, beyond, what was unmistakably the Road to Jericho. The detail of the modelling was so precise and so patiently wrought that we might have been there, two thousand years ago. But we were there. This was the difference. Were we what Katharine had found missing in Jerusalem? We were not looking at an empty shell of buildings, pavements, an empty landscape. The place was filled with people, and it was ourselves we saw. Unmistakably that was Mr Jackson, the sacristan, standing on the street corner in prayer. You didn't need to ask what he was saying, his face said it for you, 'Thank God I am not as other men'.

'Look, there's poor, mad Norman lying injured at the side of the road', said one of the children. 'And Mrs Habib from the sweet-shop is helping him. Why is the vicar crossing the road, Mummy?'

People stood around in groups in animated argument about themselves. It was nauseating to watch those who gloated over another's exposure. Don't you think she has got the bank manager just right as Zacchaeus? I always did say what a *little* man he is. Their scoffing and I-told-you-soing would rise to a great crescendo of finger-pointing and squawking until suddenly their eyes came to rest upon themselves. One had become so hysterical about it all that he actually began to cry when he recognised himself, beneath the olive trees, greeting Jesus with a kiss.

No. You are right. Jesus did not resemble any of us.

There was a squeal, or was it a scream – at least, I have never heard anything quite like it in church before – when Mrs Smith recognised herself as the scantily clad woman on the ground, about to be stoned by two men, Mr Scroggins and Tony Tubbs of the parochial church council, who were wielding rocks above their heads. Her initial response was simply one of embarrassment at being portrayed *en déshabille* for all the parish to see, but when the full import of the story was brought home to her, with evident pleasure, by Mrs Wainwright, she was hopping mad and began to protest her innocence with a lot of effing and blinding. When she fetched her husband he came storming over and punched Mr Scroggins (why didn't he hit Mrs Carpenter?) on the nose. 'Don't let the blood drip on the model', I said, feebly. Then someone hit Mr Smith, and a scuffle broke out with men on the floor and the crowd drew back like the waters of the Red Sea. It was just like being in the school playground again, with the Bishop, who had been a rugby blue, playing the part of teacher.

The vicar, under pressure from many angry parishioners, proposed closing the exhibition until the model could be removed from the church, but the Bishop made a speech which was eloquent and decisive in its old-fashionedness. The gist was that it was good that we should dwell together in unity, face up to our differences with love and honesty, and show a strong and united front to the world.

I should have told you that Mrs Carpenter had not omitted herself from the tableau. Why should she? She is not that kind of person. She and I and three others were to be seen down at the hardware shop filling our lamps with oil, while the bridegroom was arriving on horseback outside the banqueting hall. I ask you, foolish virgins! Elspeth would laugh at that.

Furthermore, not all of the characters were what you might call, for want of a better word, bad. Apart from the wedding guest who wasn't dressed properly, the rich young man stalking shamefacedly away, the tax collectors and Pharisees, and those who were too busy with their brides, yokes of oxen, or rent collection to accept the king's invitation to his feast, there were those who were not unflattered by, so to say, the part they got.

Apart from Mrs Habib, there were the penitents, like Johnny Semopoulos as the prodigal son, and Debbie (I forget her other name) anointing Jesus' feet. There were those with faith: the centurion, and the Syro-Phoenician woman. And those who had used their talents well.

It was during the fracas involving Mr and Mrs Smith that the television crew arrived, one man brandishing a blindingly bright light, alongside a pair of trainers and tight jeans supporting a camera that stalked us like a tiger after its prey. I think it was the light's glare more than anything else that stopped the fighting. The vicar strode up to the man with the microphone, who asked for Mr Carpenter. 'I think you must mean *Mrs* Carpenter', replied the vicar.

Many of us were interviewed, and there was no shortage of people pushing forward to express their indignation. Eventually the vicar persuaded a reluctant Mrs Carpenter to come forward.

We all watched her on the 'Nine O'Clock News' that night. Wasn't this an insensitive, even *unchristian*, contribution to a church celebration, the interviewer asked? She spoke slowly and quietly, often covering her mouth with her hand, as she always did, in an effort to disguise the lisp. She led the interviewer to the model. If you look carefully, she explained, and no one has yet given me the chance to demonstrate this, I have designed the heads so that they are all interchangeable. Any one of them can sit on another body without any incongruity. You see, we are not the people we think we are. And she swiftly, almost imperceptibly, switched Mr Jackson's head with that of the good and faithful servant who had used his ten talents wisely, where it fitted perfectly.

She was right, I thought to myself, we are not the people we think we are. We wear our masks like onion skins; peel off one and there is another underneath, and then another. But God knows who we are. What makes us look at ourselves? Oh, we are looking at ourselves all the time. That's what distinguishes us from the animals, this talent for self-regarding. Show a dog a mirror and it will bark at its own reflection, angry that another dog is in the room. Or if it is intelligent will look behind the glass to find its enemy. But give a person a mirror and they will preen and pose until they have convinced themselves that they are the person they think they are.

The interviewer, however, pressed this point. Didn't she, nevertheless, regret what she had done? Would she have to move out of the neighbourhood?

Why should I? And as she spoke she continued to change all the heads around. I believe that God is the one who knows truly who we are, and if we put our trust in him, he will show us who we are, not only helping us to recognise our faults, but as importantly, helping us to recognise our potential. And we don't really need to look further than the model village of the gospels to find out.

So this model is a kind of sermon to the people of St Mark's? With an impish smile she replied that, yes, if he cared to put it that way, it was.

I still sometimes think about that evening and the interview which, judging by the letters the vicar and the BBC received, made such an impact on the public. But also of the embarrassment of seeing Mr Carpenter in the background, grinning, waving at the camera, and licking his lips like a cartoon cat.

# Quite a Chat

Henry Crimond died of cancer. He had been a pillar of the church for forty years: sidesman, financial guru, member of the parochial church council, encourager of harassed vicars. Genial in life and practical about death, this ripe apple had left £250 for 'the cheerful and spirited entertainment of my friends and relations after my funeral'. Henry's shot at life after death? His own messianic banquet – a binge in the parish hall.

The pin-striped funeral conductor gave a dignified but oddly inappropriate bow to Henry's mortal remains, and the bearers, hurriedly forsaking cigarettes and conversations about their weekends, took up the coffin with professional propriety.

'Jesus said, I am the resurrection and I am the life; he who believes in me, though he die, yet shall he live, and whoever lives and believes in me shall never die.'

I had spoken to Henry about this moment two weeks ago, when the surgeon had told him that he had only a short time to live. Cancer of the pancreas is insidious and difficult to treat effectively. Henry lay propped up by pillows, his fruity features beginning obviously to shrink, eyes sinking into their dark grey sockets, and said, 'Well, Vicar. The quack has given me my marching orders.' He tried to look his defiant look, but that old mask couldn't cover fear. We looked at each other for a time, hesitantly, lips gesturing speech, but failing to find co-ordination. I took his hand and he gave it to me willingly, not in the hail-fellow-well-met muscular manner that I was used to from him, but softly like a woman. And through that intimate skin-to-skin contact, devoid of all the institutional formality engrained by welcoming clients and clinching deals, a new language of care, hope and vulnerability was spoken.

'I'm sorry, Henry', I said. 'Are you frightened?' Of

course he was frightened, frightened of the unknown, of pain, dying, what would happen to the family.

'I'm very worried about Connie . . . she's been . . . she's been . . .', he began to weep. I knew what he meant: his helpmeet, his lover, devoted mother of their children, his sense of proportion when the tensions of business became too much.

'A good wife', I said.

'She's a wonderful girl. I couldn't ask for better.' He paused. 'I hope that one day we shall meet again in heaven. Do you think we shall?'

'I don't know any more about heaven than you do, Henry', I said.

'But you're the priest; you're supposed to know.' He sensed my evasion, my holding back. He wanted assurance and comfortable words at this time of crisis, not a philosophical discussion. Even if his intellect cast doubts in his mind whether we should ever enjoy personal relationships after death as we do now, he wanted to hear me say that of course we shall. He wanted me to conspire with him in any way I could to ease the pain of being forced by the inexorable progress of terminal illness to part from loved ones. And I was ready to do that because I wanted him to be at peace in his soul, but I also knew him to be a practical man who liked to call a spade a spade. I thought how a few years ago, when he was active in local affairs, from governing schools to membership of the philatelic society, he had stood up and told the church council they were hypocrites, because they refused to give money to an international charity for fear it would end up as guns for freedom fighters. Now, despite the dark-blue suit, and half-rimmed spectacles perched on a spreading nose beneath bushy eyebrows, Henry was not the reactionary suburbanite he appeared. They were hypocrites, he said with a disarming smile, and in moderated tones, because they were using a half-baked political excuse to justify their basic selfishness, hidden under the great escape clause, charity begins at home.

'I believe our risen bodies will be different from our physical bodies', I continued. 'I agree with St Paul when he says that what is buried a physical body will be raised a spiritual body.'

'But we shall recognise each other?'

'Perhaps we shall recognise each other by our personalit-
ies rather than by physical characteristics. I mean if we are
to keep our physical bodies after death, at what age and in
what condition would they be resurrected? Would the physically handicapped person be handicapped for ever? Do you
think that the soldier who has had a leg blown off in war
will go around on crutches in heaven?'

'I see your point', he said, examining the back of his
hands, which had become skeletal like an illustration of meta-
carpals and phalanges in a medical textbook. 'I am beginning
to think it might not be such a bad thing to get rid of this
worn-out old body and swap it in for a new one.'

'I heard a professor of theology on the radio the other
night saying that St Thomas Aquinas, who was a very fat
man, believed that at the resurrection everyone would be
medium-sized and aged about thirty.'

He smiled. 'Thirty was a nice age to be.' He suddenly
seemed drowsy and gazed into the space above him, as if
the air were full of memories revolving round the yellow
lampshade and the light bulb, which burned unnecessarily
in the spring sunshine.

He let go my hand and reached for the bedside table
like a blind man, knocking over a teacup. 'Somewhere there
you'll find an envelope', he said. I took it and wiped off the
drops of tea that had blurred my name. 'You keep it. Those
are the instructions for my funeral. No, don't open it now.
Wait until I'm . . . until I've gone.'

The silence was renewed. It is in the nature of such
conversations to be spasmodic and hesitant. Words are
treacherous and have to be chosen; too many are not only
tiring, but can suffocate the expression of thought and fears,
which are brought reluctantly to the surface, in case they
should seem silly or childish. Besides, the meeting of priest
and patient in these circumstances is not so much a matter
of explanations, as an empathetic being together – of which
perhaps the holding of hands is the sacrament. How often
after such a visit a person says that they have been helped
or have found peace of mind, when the actual conversation
if written down would only seem banal. The principal value
of words here for Henry was to say out loud that he was
dying, and to hear himself saying it. He wanted to release
the thoughts that had been swirling round in his mind with

such turbulence, into physical, audible sounds. It was like casting out a demon. While friends and relations had been looking on the bright side, and hoping that he would get out and about in the better weather, Henry had put on a brave face, but all the time he wanted to shout out: I shan't be here, I shall be dead.

'I want to be cremated. I suppose you think that's wrong.' There was a pale glint in his yellow-grey eye as he tried to spar in his old jovial way. Or was this the expression of another uncertainty?

'It was legalised in 1885, you know.'

'What?'

'Cremation. Of course I see no religious objection. If you believe in a spiritual resurrection, the body doesn't matter any more and should be disposed of as conveniently as possible. And if you believe in the eventual reconstitution of the physical body, it is such a miracle that it must be equally possible to achieve whatever the nature of a person's remains.'

The half-hour we had spent together had clearly been an effort for him, in the sense that he had fought off physical discomfort and the soporific effect of the morphia. He now began to sink more heavily into the sheets and pillows.

'Shall we say a prayer before I go?' I asked. He nodded. I felt imprisoned by my inadequacy and inability to find the right words, but I knew that that was an inappropriately self-conscious response, and that God copes where human resources fail.

'O God, our Father; we pray that Henry may be surrounded by your healing love and power. Give him courage and faith as he approaches death. . . . We thank you for all the support and love he has received from Connie over the years, and especially during the recent months. We commend her, and Joyce, to your fatherly care . . .'

'And my grandchildren, Mark and Samantha', whispered Henry. His head lay back in serious contemplation, something like an effigy on a tomb, but real, not a forgotten piece of history in stone. Taking the phial of oil, which he had knocked over when fumbling for the envelope, I dipped the tip of my thumb into the oil, and made the sign of the cross on his forehead, drawing the marks slowly over the crevices and cracks of his skin, which appeared to me as through a magnifying glass as I try to give all my attention to this real slogger of a Christian pilgrim. I am starkly aware of the privilege of this unfamiliar intimacy of physical closeness. I could have leant forward and kissed his brow, should have done. 'I anoint you in the name of Our Lord Jesus Christ. May our heavenly Father grant you the inward anointing of his Holy Spirit, the Spirit of strength, and joy, and peace. The blessing of God Almighty, the Father, the Son, and the Holy Spirit, be with you evermore. Amen.'

Downstairs in the neat living-room, verdant with indoor plants as pampered as the Yorkshire terrier, Connie had sat on the sofa acting out the reading of a magazine. What was she thinking? She must have been listening, waiting for the stair to creak, because as I reached the hall she was up, looking enquiringly, wanting to make tea. The ritual of warming the pot and reaching for the biscuit tin is a useful diversion when conversation is on edge. She was younger by some years – in her early sixties, well groomed, strong hair streaked with magenta, making a virtue out of greyness, her fine features drawn by anxiety, slim and elegant in a straight skirt and white blouse, square and frilled at the neck.

'It was kind of you to come', she said. 'I know how busy you must be, but he especially wanted to see you.'

'How are you?' I asked. I could see her hand shake as she poured the tea.

'Oh, I'm fine. The doctor's coming at four o'clock. He has given me some sleeping tablets, but I don't want to get my sleep that way. Did Henry talk? He's hardly been with it the last few days.'

'Yes, we had quite a chat.'

She looked relieved. She had obviously hoped, as she thumbed through her magazine, that in the room above there had been a great unravelling of mysteries, a putting of the spiritual house in order, the administration of a skill and knowledge which far transcended what consultants and solicitors and concerned neighbours had to offer. And although outside in the business-as-usual street I experienced a dazed sense of platitudinous incompetence (quite a chat), maybe she was right. An effective steward of the mysteries of God rarely knows himself to be such at the time. I hoped that in this case love had triumphed over reason, and that the peace of God which passes all understanding had been mediated through the sacrament.

Henry died three days later.

# Sometimes It Causes Me To Tremble

This central section is not a story, unless you were to say it is the story of how, at present, I understand the Passion of Jesus Christ. I think it is important to put in that proviso 'at present' because ideas develop and our minds move on.

I am standing in the Ashmolean Museum looking at an enamelled sixteenth-century plaque of the crucifixion by Pierre Raymond of Limoges. It is only seven inches by nine, and the workmanship is exquisite – vibrant blues and greens offset with browns and gold. Behind the crucified figure of Christ is a golden-turreted castle, like a house of many mansions; beneath his feet a mêlée of soldiers, spears, shields, shying horses and women. Perhaps I also hear the music of the Mozart Requiem. I imagined myself on Calvary. What questions go through my mind. Why? How could they do it? Who is the victim? What did he think? Is there an answer? Why am I trembling?

## WHY CRUCIFY JESUS?

When recently I received a dressing down from a diocesan official for failing to get planning permission for a repair to the fabric of my church, since everyone (including the diocese's own advisory committee) agreed it was a great improvement, I was tempted to write a reply which would read simply:

Dear Diocesan Official,

Have you forgotten? The sabbath was made for man, not man for the sabbath.

Yours etc.

– until I realised that such action would be so provocative that the matter could only end up in the Chancellor's court.

Small examples like this, which are no doubt experienced in all walks of life, help us to see how Jesus' attitude to the Pharisaic establishment of his time must have provoked great anger. Basically, he was questioning the priorities of the whole established order. As early as chapter 2 in Mark's gospel there is a series of stories describing confrontations between Jesus and the Jewish authorities. Jesus is accused by the scribes of blasphemy because he tells a paralytic that his sins are forgiven. Next, the Pharisees ask complainingly why he eats with tax-collectors and sinners. Then they criticise his disciples for breaking the sabbath law by plucking ears of corn. This is followed, in the first paragraph of chapter 3, by a battle of wills over the proposed healing on the sabbath of a man who has a withered hand. The Pharisees stand in wait to accuse Jesus of working on the sabbath, and he exposes their nit-picking legalism by asking whether it is lawful on the sabbath to do good or to do harm, to save life or to kill. Mark tells us that the Pharisees went out and immediately held counsel with the Herodians against him, how to destroy him. It seems unlikely that there would have been plots to kill him at the very beginning of his Galilean ministry, but this group of stories, and the establishment's response to them, illustrate the typical grounds on which the authorities eventually did bring him to trial.

Even as we hear these stories we naturally side with Jesus against the scribes and Pharisees, whom we cast in the role of baddies. Yet we would see things differently, I am certain, if Jesus were conducting his ministry in our society, and it were our values that were being exposed by his teaching.

In our spirituality we are taught to think of Jesus as a friend and support, one who accepts us as we are, which is a true but certainly not exclusive picture of his relationship with us. For it is perfectly obvious that, rather than bringing peace of mind, his ministry was a threat to many. Insecurity of lifestyle was what he offered to would-be followers – sell all that you have and follow me; let the dead bury their own dead; anyone who turns his hand to the plough and looks back is not fit for the Kingdom of God. This threatening insecurity was also what he offered to society in general. He *might* have said, I came to upset the status quo, and to set you self-righteous blustering and spluttering into your beards. He did say, I have not come to bring peace on earth, but a sword.

It is almost perverse the way he turns everything on its head, as if he were trying to annoy people on purpose. The last shall be first and the first shall be last. He who would be great among you must become the servant of all. Unless you become as little children you cannot enter the Kingdom of heaven. He who would save his life must lose it. What's he talking about, you can hear them saying. The man's mad. He's possessed by the demons he casts out. And you can't blame them. We spend our lives sorting out an acceptable social framework in which to live, sifting values, trying to do the best for our children, agonising about the needs of the poor, following the will of God as laid down in our ancient scriptures, trying to be good. And he comes along and tells us we're no better than murderers, adulterers, exploiters and racists. Who does he think he is? Wandering about like a down-and-out, cadging meals from strangers, mixing with the riff-raff, and abusing the hospitality of his friends. Is he trying to sabotage our religion, the blasphemer?

Yes. The bland assumption that we are on the side of Jesus leaves us open to attack. We soon become tetchy when our own motives are put in the spotlight, especially when we have tried hard to be model citizens, and believe that our lives are built on the rock of Christian morality. Think how fiercely the established middle-class in our society defends its so-called freedoms – for example, the right to buy private education, or private medicine, or to earn five and six times as much as the poorly paid. But I am being rewarded for my skills, my responsibility, my talent. Think how we tend to look at the homeless alcoholics not as people but as a plague on the streets, or drug-takers as scum, AIDS victims as deserving all they get, football hooligans, ticket touts, pimps, punks, and others who do not fit into a pattern of comfortable relationship as social lepers. And imagine what Jesus would have to say about our attitude and about the repentence we should undertake. But the man's a dangerous subversive. He's a looney, a lefty, unrealistic. If we follow his policies society will end up in disorder and chaos.

And such easy dismissive talk quickly turns to anger when the agitator begins to attract a group of supporters around him, and the threat to the status quo becomes real.

We don't have to look beyond contemporary times to see gruesome examples of the same kind of violence that killed Christ: a priest murdered in Poland by the secret police for preaching in favour of Solidarity; the archbishop Oscar Romero shot in front of thousands of people as he celebrated mass in the poignantly named country of El Salvador (the saviour). Romero had said in a sermon on the feast of Corpus Christi: 'It is most opportune to pay homage to the body and blood of the Son of Man, while there are so many outrages to his body and blood among us. I should like to join this homage of our faith to the presence of the body and blood of Christ, which we have shed, with all the blood shed, and the corpses piled up, here in our own land and throughout the world.'

And he did pay homage with his own blood.

A similar anger was evident in Britain after the Falklands War memorial service, when the prayers emphasised concern for the needs of the Argentinians, their dead and wounded, which was felt by some in government to be an implicit criticism of their policy. It wasn't that those who felt angered were men and women without compassion, but that they wholeheartedly believed that they had acted bravely and justly in defending democracy – they were proud – and to hear the Christian proclamation that there is a yet more glorious way, involving forgiveness and reconciliation, is very galling.

The problem with Jesus Christ as distinct from others who have died for their faith is, we believe, that he reveals the righteousness of God. And genuine righteousness can be as threatening as genuine talent. Righteousness offends us when we are not ourselves the righteous one. It makes us jealous that we do not possess self-evident goodness and talent like this man.

To put it another way, we find it hard to bear the exaltation of a goodness which we admire, when we know ourselves to be bad. And we particularly like to expose chinks in the armour of goodness because somehow other people's failure makes our sinfulness more tolerable. For example, possibly you have experienced that sense of shameful pleasure when some great person is removed from his pedestal by illness, or scandal, even by a totally libellous hatchet job in the gutter press. Ah, but, we say, where there's smoke there's fire. How the mighty are fallen. And the seed of mob violence is sown, almost an unspoken conspiracy between inferiors to do down the one who has presumed to rise above us. And this can entangle us in a net of immoral behaviour that would shock us at an individual level.

At its very worst we have seen the force of mob violence in episodes like the Tottenham riot in 1985, when a policeman was murdered outside a block of flats on the Broadwater Farm estate, and on our television screens when two soldiers were dragged from a car in Belfast and killed in 1988. There is a terrible part of the human psyche that can suddenly lose control in a frenzy of mob violence, which expresses itself not only physically, but more often in violence of attitude of mind. I am thinking of the violence of corporate prejudice which can happily chuck the weak into the social dustbin, or the public hypocrisy which so readily hounds a person from office for sexual behaviour which half the stone-throwers indulge in themselves.

In the Sermon on the Mount, Jesus said that this kind of anger and aggression is just as bad as murder itself. It is irrational, often paranoid, and builds up to a crisis of orgasmic violence and excitement which when over leaves a sense of emptiness, of shame, of regret, of futility. Far better to work for reconciliation and forgiveness. The crucifixion seems to have been motivated by violence of this kind, and in the aftermath of shame and emptiness at least one man, the soldier standing by, recognises the graciousness of Christ's death – truly this man was a son of God.

## HOW COULD THEY DO IT?

Having talked about why Jesus was crucified, I now want to say something briefly about how he was crucified – not about the method or the physiological facts of crucifixion – but more the question of how a group of human beings can treat another human being like that.

For the past two years in my church I have chosen the Negro spiritual 'Were you there when they crucified my Lord?' as one of the hymns for the Good Friday meditation, and on both occasions have received a surprising number of criticisms for doing so. I couldn't quite understand why. Was it simply that the musical genre is culturally alien, and we don't like singing songs with choruses? Did some regard it as sentimentalising what is arguably the most sacred day in the Church's calendar? Or is there a deeper psychological reason? Is it that our liturgical framework and the rest of the hymns that we sing allow us to distance ourselves from the events of Good Friday, to be onlookers, outsiders? Do we, like Pilate, want to wash our hands and be innocent of this man's blood? Or to blame it on the Jews, as the gospels are accused of doing, and as Passion plays have often done? Whereas the Negro spiritual, this song of oppressed black slaves, pushes us right into the heart of darkness, identifying us with the evil that murdered the God of Love.

> Were you there when they nailed him to the tree?
> O sometimes it causes me to tremble, tremble, tremble;
> Were you there when they nailed him to the tree?

Have we so institutionalised our theological ideas: sin and redemption, God's love, guilt, penitence, emotion, forgiveness, reconciliation, responsibility, hope and grace, that we no longer have feelings about our religion strong enough to make us *tremble*? Has our religion been reduced to the smooth and acceptable, become, as you might say, ever so civilised? Perhaps it was precisely this subtle process of institutionalisation that numbed the sensitivities of those who actually did hammer the nails into Jesus' hands and feet, and hear his screams and see his mouth dry and twisted in agony.

I want to quote an extended passage from the novel *Her Story* by Dan Jacobson, where he is describing the thoughts of the mother of one of the thieves who was crucified beside Jesus, because it seems to me that he has recognised a truth that we often fail to see.

> It was not quick. It was not soon over. It took almost the whole day. The atrocity was attended with formalities of all kinds. Afterwards it was easier for you to recollect how these had gone than anything else you saw that day. Yes, they were intended to dignify what was being done, precisely because the important men had ordained it, and the flunkeys and blackguards who carried it out were human, too, as human as those they were torturing and even they, safe in the positions they occupied, bolstered by precedent and law, by orders from above and pressures from below, knew what an abomination they were committing. Of course they knew it. But that

did nothing to make them relent or turn away or refuse to carry on. Instead they tried to turn themselves into actors in a drama or figures in a tableau – not men responsible for what they did, not creatures with their own motives and feelings. Or if they had feelings, then they were only those which were most dutiful and severe, and therefore least reprehensible. Did they not make manifest the dignity of the state in parading these rags of men through the streets; and then, in due order, handing them over, with the appropriate declarations, to the next arm or organ of authority; and did it not, in its turn, show itself to be of an equivalent or even higher dignity in accepting, after the requisite sealings and stampings, all the obligations placed upon it?

That was how it was done. That was how they hid from themselves what they were doing, even in the very lust and excitement of doing it, and how they managed to enjoy also the forms of these concealments too. There was no end within them to such secret entanglements of pleasure and shame, of display and denial.

So, just as the Romans institutionalised and dramatised violence, passing the buck from one department to another, in order to make the outrageous acceptable, so we are tempted to formalise our relationship with Christ because we want his saving grace, but not the challenge that threatens to change our lives. It is natural enough.

We would, as it turns out in practice, be very happy for Christ to be the scapegoat – we project all our sins on to the good man and let him carry them away into the wilderness, there to die in expiation for our sins.

The whole purpose of the ritual of the scapegoat is that we don't have to go with him. He carries our burden away. He is a sort of Jonah figure. It is expedient that one man should die for the people. We can turn our back on him, desert him, leave him. This is exactly how Christ was left in the Garden of Gethsemane when the disciples fled.

## WHO WAS THE VICTIM?
## A PORTRAIT OF THE DIVINE ARTIST

The trouble with Christianity, said the student, is that it easily degenerates into mindless sentimentality. Too often it is a self-centred emotional crutch, deadening my senses to the harsh realities of the world, and the pain of my own spiritual conflicts. Read out the overhead projector to our Overhead Protector. (If you want to know what that means, just think of a congregation swaying to a syrupy chorus.) Even the idea that we are saved from our sins through Christ's passion and resurrection seems a dogma that is out of date.

Well, there's the view of an intelligent young person. What am I to say? How does God set about dealing with the self-regarding sin of his beautiful, free creatures? By showing greater humility than we ourselves are able. I take up the New Testament and read, 'Christ . . . though he was in the form of God, did not count equality with God a thing to be grasped, but emptied himself, taking the form of a servant' (Philippians 2.6ff.). So says St Paul as he grapples with the problem that if God did indeed become man in the person of Jesus Christ, how did he manage to squeeze his godliness into limited human form? He answers the dilemma with the argument that God emptied himself.

The student shrugs his shoulders and accuses theology of sophisticated theorising, remote. But emptied himself of what?

Wealth, power. He started life in a cattle-shed, slept in a manger. And then, as Paul says, he took the form of a servant. Quite a contrast, eh, to the Old Testament picture of a macho God where kingship, military strength and epic power provide the easy analogies, shaped by a very human view of greatness. Nevertheless understandable analogies. Because when we encounter God we recognise his mightiness and want to paint him in pictures taken from our worldly experience of wealth and power, so that he becomes a princely figure. But God emptied himself of these things and what was left was a brilliant distillation of godliness, a self-effacing talent for goodness. This is a style of divine leadership that is bound to be unpopular with those who want to acquire status by basking in his reflected glory. It's ironical, really, isn't it, that the thing God's most famous for, creative love, has little to do with assertive power, and everything to do with pain and effort and self-giving. Not that I want to make creativity sound whingeingly masochistic, of course not. But its pleasure is not straightforward. So many parables of life illustrate that: from the sacrifices parents make for their children to the disciplined self-sacrifice of art, like the unrecognised musical genius composing himself to death in a garret room.

Perhaps this last illustration needs a little explanation. Iris Murdoch, for example, is one of those who argue that selfish fantasy is the enemy of art and that 'to silence and expel self, to contemplate and delineate nature with a clear eye, is not easy and demands a moral discipline. A great artist is, in respect of his work, a good man, and, in a true sense, a free man.' She makes the point even more clearly by quoting what Rilke said in admiration of the painter Cézanne: he did not paint 'I like it', he painted 'there it is'.

So that's it, is it, says the student, looking sceptical. God is a man with a temperament for martyrdom, and very low self-esteem. A manic-depressive artistic sort?

I protest that I am only doing my best to explore the mystery of God with a bit of imagination and the limited linguistic tools available to me.

Since the early centuries of Christianity Christians have tried to do this. They puzzled for example about how Christ could be the embodiment of perfect God and perfect man. It's a question that demands a balancing act, putting as much godliness and as much humanity as you can on to the scales without the one overturning the other.

Take the claim that Jesus Christ was morally perfect. Now if that is true, did his moral perfection stem from the fact that he was God, and therefore automatically incapable of sin, or did it come from somewhere else? I believe that part of God's self-emptying was that he emptied himself of moral perfection in order to become man. Because no human being could be convincing without being dominated by the so-called 'selfish gene' – the genetic obsession with survival, the inbuilt mechanism for self-protection. As an infant he must have cried for his milk, been irritable when his mother couldn't understand exactly where he felt the pain of an illness. The one recorded incident of his childhood suggests a precocity that is distinctly unattractive – all very well to sparkle in front of the theologians, but what about his distraught parents? What of the commandment to honour your father and your mother? Surely it's not good enough simply to point a finger to the sky and say to Mary and Joseph, poor things, 'Wist ye not that I be about my Father's business'. Or in adulthood, in the wilderness, surely, the temptations are real, not just a dramatic device on the part of the gospel writers. And for temptations to be real, there must be the genuine possibility of falling for them. So he must have thought, for example, when his gut was grinding with hunger, this self-imposed religious discipline of fasting is ridiculous. And when I am trying to raise support for my ministry, why don't I seduce the crowds with a few tricks? Besides, you can always make out a case for the end justifying the means. As for dispossession, why should my own Jewish people suffer any longer the occupation of their land by crude soldiers and exploiters, abusing their women, forcing them to carry their baggage, eating their best food? Do I really believe what I say that the meek shall inherit the earth? I mean is it really true?

Then the final and climactic temptation before his arrest to cut and run – Father, if it is your will, take this cup from me. The selfish gene must have worked very hard indeed over that one: don't be a fool, don't let them kill you. You are more use alive. You are only thirty-three years old. Do you really not want to drink wine again with your friends, enjoy their laughter, sitting up late putting the world to rights? In the case of all those temptations it was perfectly possible that Jesus might have given in.

I think you rather wish he had, said the student, hoping for mischief. You want to find a chink in the armour. Anyway I thought the whole thing was pre-planned. You know, God decides to bring the salvation of his people to a climax by visiting them himself. If God is God, he must have known exactly what he was up to.

I'm sorry. I just don't think that God is as unsubtle as that. (And, yes, you are right. I do wish he had given in, in a perverse kind of way. Just as I wish Mozart had lived thirty years longer. But if Jesus Christ had given in, then his story would never have been written.)

As for that old chestnut, destiny, the devil wants us to think that an event of history was always inevitable simply because it happened. We read back destiny into the life of Christ in such a way that we come to think it was God's purpose to suffer as he did right from the start. And, of course, there are many biblical references which are interpreted retrospectively as prefiguring the crucifixion.

But don't you think that perhaps those prophecies show

how God gradually reveals his nature, not that he always had Calvary in mind. It is crucially important to recognise in the incarnation that God accepted a place in the free world which he had created, and subjected himself to its changes and chances. Christ's achievement, is seems to me, is to embody the most holy and perfect encounter experienced between God and man. It is like the blending of imagination and discipline in art, or the mysterious mix of self-renunciation and possessive desire in love. Jesus, the man, showed how absolute obedience to God is possible. And his moral perfection is to be found in his ability as an adult to overcome the pressing attentions of the selfish gene.

As he moved around Galilee and Jerusalem he didn't like what he saw. He hated to see people disfigured by leprosy, lame, blind, begging, outcast. He revealed God's desire to give wholeness of life to his people by representative action, healing the sick and identifying with the sufferers even by touching the untouchables. But there was no final solution to the problem except to accept it, to experience it for himself, and in doing so to demonstrate the self-giving love of God, which is ready to go to the limits of his endurance to be at one with his people.

Jesus' life unfolded in response to situations; it wasn't pre-planned by God – now we'll heal a paralytic, then we'll raid the Temple, then we'll be crucified. God emptied himself of the luxury of any preconceived plan. He simply gave himself to human life, and then extemporised, like a talented musician. He took the raw material of life as he found it, and turned it as it were into art. Neither should we imagine that because he was God this was for him a matter of effortless ease, nonchalantly doing what came naturally. It was always costly, in the way that we find the development of any talent to be costly, whether it is for brain surgery or housework, loving or writing, scholarship or football.

Jesus sometimes taught by comparison: if human beings are capable of such and such virtue, how much more do you think God is capable of it? I knew a junior surgeon who told me how he had assisted his consultant at a very complicated operation on an accident victim. The operation lasted seven hours, and when it was over, the consultant had spent so much concentration and energy that he had to be led from the theatre like a blind man. Imagine how much more costly our salvation is to God.

Student: Don't you think the time has come for you to tell me how salvation works?

I could only reply by quoting God's challenge to Job:

'Where were you when I laid the foundation of the earth? Tell me if you have understanding . . . Can you bind the chains of the Pleiades, or loose the cords of Orion. . . . Do you give the horse his might, or clothe his neck with strength. . . . Shall a faultfinder contend with the Almighty?'

We struggle to find language adequate to express the mystery of what the eye of faith sees to be true – namely that somehow through his Passion Jesus Christ puts us in a new relationship with God. In trying to answer the question, Paul played the scriptures at their own game by saying that Christ was the New Adam who reversed the sin of the old Adam. In the Garden of Eden Adam had caused mankind's fall from grace by eating the forbidden fruit of the tree of the knowledge of good and evil. Before that disobedience Adam and Eve had been like gods, afterwards they were mortal. As in Adam all die, even so in Christ shall all be made alive. There's a tradition that the Garden of Eden and Calvary were one and the same place. John Donne in his poem 'Hymne to God my God', says:

We think that paradise and calvarie
Christ's Crosse, and Adam's tree, stood in one place;
Look Lord, and finde both Adams met in me;
As the first Adam's sweat surrounds my face,
May the last Adam's blood my soule embrace.

So, in an ironic way, Christ is nailed to the tree of the knowledge of good and evil and thus cancels out the sin which changed Adam and Eve's life of paradise into the daily grind of survival against pain and the elements.

But let me suggest a new image. Not an explanation, just an idea. As Jesus Christ, God made man, accepts dispossession; as he empties himself; as he denies himself, and goes to the limit of his endurance for his creation, it is as if the denial-of-self creates a vacuum into which the pressure of grace is forced to rush. The vacuum of selflessness makes an ideal space for the Holy Spirit. This is surely what it means

to be open to the Holy Spirit – the rushing mighty wind.
Or put it this way. The passion of Jesus creates an enormous
pressure of spiritual energy which is itself the impetus of the
resurrection. As Jesus repeatedly rejects worldly values and
expectations, it is like a valve withdrawing down a cylinder,
building up a massive vacuum which has to be filled with
the resurrection.

We have seen the power of this kind of passive resistance
and self-denial in the lives of other leaders – Gandhi is an
obvious example – and it has teased us with its subtlety. It
doesn't come naturally because the power of the selfish gene
has to be overcome. Perhaps, even, we have been irritated
by Christ's submissiveness and shared in the disappointment
of Simon the Zealot, Judas Iscariot, and Peter, as we have
read the gospel story and found Jesus refusing to lead an
uprising, failing to match popular, excited messianic expectations, running away from fame and wealth, not even allow-
ing Peter to defend him in the Garden of Gethsemane. And
wouldn't it have been marvellous if, when those despicable
loud-mouths taunted him with the words, if you are the son
of God, save yourself and come down from the cross, he had
come down and confounded the High Priest and those feeble
Roman puppets.

But reflection tells me us that he chose the more godly
way. His submission to the sacrifice of love renders impotent
the conventional forms of political and social coercion which
try to destroy him, questions their moral integrity, and sows
the seed of self-examination in the minds of those whose job
it is to enforce political power.

As it was, the Jewish and Roman authorities knew they
were on shaky ground – they had killed a man who had
committed no crime simply because he had touched the raw
nerve of their religious hypocrisy, or, in the case of the
Romans, simply because he was a nuisance. Therefore after
the institutional violence had been done, the consequent
sense of guilt and self-questioning would have been part of
the cumulative energy of the resurrection.

I would like to believe, but you fail to convince me, said
the student. So we decided to call it a day and I comforted
myself with the thought that no one is ever argued into the
Kingdom of God.

## WHAT DID HE THINK?

But wait a minute. Am I writing a poem? Do theologians only write poems and paint pictures about the crucifixion on the grand scale of Leonardo and Raphael, with lashings of oil and pigment and their national landscape in the background? Do they try to write history on the cosmic scale, universalising from the particular, and miss the actual moment of history, the feeble, sad, terrible, lonely, isolated moment of history?

Is it really a blasphemy to imagine what Christ thought on the cross? Did Martin Scorsese in *The Last Temptation of Christ* commit some awful crime against the Holy Spirit? Or do we not, out of our compassion, owe Christ a thought for what he suffered? Can we not come down from the grand pinnacle of theological speculation to the wounds themselves?

He suddenly remembered the man with the stoop and the unpleasant breath. The man who egged him on with all the lucidity and persuasiveness of a politician who knew he was right. The one who wanted to build up the resistance, form cells, stash arms, mobilise guerrilla forces, train them to harsh standards of aggression and commitment. If it hadn't been for him he might not be here now. No that was crazy. Of course they would have framed him anyway, picked him up any time. The authorities were not stupid, but they wanted that little animator of subversity in their pocket too. He could see the manic eyes sparkling now, one-track-minded, anything for the cause. He'd even sell his soul to the devil. What hurt him was the betrayal, and that he must love the betrayer with all his mind, and with all his soul, and all his strength, even while his nerves were sending currents of excruciating torture to every inch of his body. Men had been known to bite out their own tongues in crucifixion for the very pain.

## THE FUTURE?

In his novel *The Unbearable Lightness of Being*, Milan Kundera wrote: 'People usually escape from their troubles into the future; they draw an imaginary line across the path of time, a line beyond which current troubles will cease to exist'. He was writing about Czechoslovakia after the Russian invasion, a sort of action replay of Roman-occupied Palestine, a parable of the remorseless cycle of political history.

People usually escape from their troubles into the future. We know that that is not entirely true; some try to escape from their troubles into the past, which is at best a rosy nostalgia, and at worst a recipe for mental illness, as a person obsessively retells the particular fragment of their story which haunts them, from which they are unable to escape: a promising university career that ended in failure, or a love affair that came to nothing, one morsel of idealised happiness. At least to escape into the future shows that a person has hope, sees possibilities, hasn't given in to despair. And although in the quotation escape implies weakness, it has to be said that so long as we live in this temporal order, openness to the future is a necessary virtue, a constituent part of faith, without which growth would be stunted and the present would die.

There can be little doubt that the Jewish messianic dream of Jesus' time was centred on the future. In the Bible the people in Israel are chosen by God. But being chosen is a dangerous game, because there is always the possibility of being rejected. For the Jews God's promise is established through the story of the Exodus and the journey to the Promised Land. Then all this is frustrated by the Babylonian conquest and their subsequent exile from their holy place. They experience repeated humiliation at the hands of alien powers, not least of course the Romans, and the consequence was the development of a story of good times coming when the burden of physical sickness would be lifted, when the palmy days of the Kingdom of David would be restored, and even nature itself would be at peace – the lion would lie down with the lamb. Jewish spirituality is developed to a very large degree through the courage and hope shown in adversity. To what degree, though, should it be criticised as escape into the future?

Did Jesus draw that imaginary line across time, beyond which his troubles would cease to exist? And when he hung on the cross did he see that line drawing mercifully closer and closer? Certainly, one of the clear indications of his limited human mind is that he seemed to think that the end of the world was coming in the immediately foreseeable future, and that belief fired his sense of the immense urgency that his message contains. But is his teaching really directed towards the future? Is it tantamount to saying: if you suffer now and deny yourself now you will be rewarded with the prize of everlasting luxury in heaven? Some of what he says seems to suggest this. Take the parable of the rich man and Lazarus, for example. In life the hard-hearted rich man ignored the misery of Lazarus whose open sores were licked by dogs. In the afterlife Lazarus lived in the lap, or at least the bosom, of luxury, while the rich man, burning in hell, was ignored, pleading that at least his brothers should be warned of the danger. Jesus never meant this brilliant little short story as a description of the future; it was an admonition about the present.

The student asked me what I thought about the future. To be more precise, how could an all-loving God consign the greater part of what he had, after all, created in his own image to the eternal rubbish heap? Is it only believing Christians who get to heaven? What about people of other religions? This time his question was open, meant, he wanted to know. It was, of course, a question expecting the answer no – no he couldn't consign the greater part of his human creation to eternal damnation; a question that hangs like the sword of Damocles over the chilling fact that so many Christians across the Christian centuries and in the present seem to delight at the prospect of spending eternity watching others burn. The God of Jairus' Daughter, the God of the Woman taken in Adultery, the self-giving God who said to the thief on the cross 'This day you will be with me in paradise', could not possibly think like that, not for all the wheat and the tares or all the sheep and the goats in the world. That is why I balk every time I reach the last paragraph in the intercessions in our liturgy: We commend ourselves and all *Christian* people to your unfailing love. I can't say it. It's too exclusive. Why only Christian people? How do you define a Christian person anyway? No one should pray that prayer, just pray for all people whoever they are and wherever they may be. I think there is the authentic voice of prophecy in Jesus' statement about the cross, 'I, if I am lifted up will draw all people to myself'. It seems to me an affirmation of the ultimate purpose of God to bring the whole of his creation into unity with himself, to express the same truth that Julian of Norwich perceived in her divine revelations that all shall be well, and all manner of thing shall be well. If that is so, then the burden of Jesus' teaching falls on the present.

Christ was a man of the here and now. Christianity is a religion of the here and now, and the greatest disservice that can be done to it is to turn it into an escape from our troubles into the future. Christ was not an escapist. He prayed for God to do what was necessary; he prayed for the coming of God's Kingdom now; he prepared people to be ready for the challenge of that Kingdom which would come like a thief in the night. Christ accepted the cross.

Of course, you might want to say that he had no choice. Quite apart from any divine considerations, once the wheels of the state were set in motion there was no stopping them in all their callous cruelty. But look at the manner of his accepting of that cruelty – full of grace and truth. You will recognise those two words, grace and truth, as belonging to St John's great hymn of the incarnation which we read at Christmas, the celebration of Jesus' birth, but we are only able to discern these godly qualities as we contemplate the manner of his dying. If you want to put it in a catchy phrase, the medium is the message. He didn't postpone the confrontation with evil to some indeterminate point in the future, he dealt with it once and for all right there and then, now, through being the person that he was, graciously, self-givingly, God.

Therefore he affects your life now. What is important is not some dream for the future, but the presence of the divine genius coming face to face with your life in this moment.


## THE WORLD IN TUNE

Henry Vaughan, the seventeenth-century Metaphysical poet, in his poem 'The Morning-watch', describes prayer as 'the world in tune'. The poem celebrates creation in a picture of the Welsh countryside where the poet lived:

> The rising winds,
> And falling springs,
> Birds, beasts, all things
> Adore him in their kinds.

It is a prayer that the soul may abide in God. The

harmonious sound of nature is an echo of heavenly bliss, and so prayer is the music of the world in harmony with God.

This idea that the order of nature reflects the existence of a beneficent creator God is common to Vaughan's time. We find a similar argument in Addison's poem 'The spacious firmament on high', which continues:

> With all the blue ethereal sky.
> And spangled heavens, a shining frame,
> Their great Original proclaim.

In today's televisual view of nature, where the idyll of a primrose-banked Welsh stream is quickly countered by shots of drought-weary villages or towns ripped up by earthquake, it is very easy to miss the insight of those who worshipped God in what seemed to them a more stable order. Surely the same theme is implicit in our prayers for peace and justice, and our concern for the ecology of the planet – worries about the ozone layer, and the hacking down of the rainforests, acid rain, the pollution of rivers and the oceans. We know very well that for life to prosper we must live harmoniously with each other and with our environment. To the Christian the source of this harmony is God, because he is the source of love and relationship. That is why it is helpful to see the root of prayer not as asking for favours from God, or harassing him with the headlines of the daily paper, but as concentration on his being, trying to get into the mind of Christ. In this sense we might say that Christ is the world in tune, because harmony is what Christ offers in a dissonant world.

However, this may seem a false image for the crucifixion. What composer of a Passion or a Requiem would represent the agony of Christ in quiet pastoral harmonious tones? He would surely represent the pain of the nails in strident discord, and the bereft cry 'My God, my God, why hast thou forsaken me?' in sounds of clashing torment. But harmony that is not contrasted with dissonance is bland, and one of the great delights of music is the resolution of discord into harmony. A composer of genius like Mozart achieves his compelling effect by surprising us with his 'crushed harmonies, glancing collisions, agonising delights' and thus enriches his music to the point where some of us have found he has created a language which reaches beyond the scope of what we can describe, exploring the limits of human understanding.

So it was at the crucifixion where, with a kind of artistic virtuosity, Christ symbolised harmonious relationship, offering a salvation that is the direct result of the self-giving nature of his own life. He is the go-between, the arbitrator, the reconciler, the champion of new relationship, and, being God, he is of course in a unique position to be so. His unspoken proclamation from the cross is: If God, the source of your being, can suffer this gross and undeserved torment because of his inexhaustible love for you, then you too can stop performing your self-regarding pirouettes.

It is in this sense that God's suffering draws the poison of sin, and in this sense that we are able to say that he has borne our griefs and carried our sorrows. As Christ's blood drains away, so sin is drained away too. But not in any magical cure-all way. The universal nature of Christ's redemptive work lies in the fact that he exposes once and for all what God is really like – universally loving. And that love conquers sin. Christ is the focus or meeting-point for resolving all the disharmonies of our human selfishness. Christ is the world in tune.

If I were to stretch my musical analogy even further, I might compare the crucifixion of Christ to the peg of a violin. The string is wound tightly round the peg and before music can be played the peg has to be tightened until the string is perfectly in tune. The period of tuning-up before a performance is cacophonous and ugly, but because of it the whole instrument is ready to combine all its potential in the creation of beauty. Of course, that beauty depends also on the skill and discipline of the player, and we are the players.

There has always been a fear amongst Christians that it is dangerous to suggest that we can in any way earn our salvation by the good we do. To believe that would be to indulge in an arrogance that is completely alien to discipleship. Rather, we should accept that salvation is entirely a free and undeserved gift that God chooses to give us. Paul said that we are justified by faith and not by works. But like all religious language, the idea of justification by faith only tells a part of the truth. Paul himself recognised the absurd situation you could get into by following the idea to its logical conclusion when he asks the rhetorical question: Shall I sin therefore, that grace may abound? In other words: I might as well be a reckless sinner in order to give God the maximum opportunity for grace. No, this is crazy!

The truth is, I think, that when we begin to discern the real cost of God's self-giving love, then we want to respond to it, because we find it irresistible and liberating. Admiration for Christ means that we want to imitate him, just as in life we meet individuals who become our heroes, mentors, formative influences, whom we wish to follow.

So I believe that Christian goodness is a reality for which we should strive and which we can achieve, but it is always motivated by our reverential love of God. That is what is distinctive about Christian ethics. It is not that we are always likely to behave differently from agnostics, humanists and others; or better than them – thankfully, compassion, kindness and consideration are qualities shared across the barriers of creed – but that love and admiration for God compels us to try to follow his example.

## WHY AM I TREMBLING?

Ever since the years when I taught A-level religious education in a north London comprehensive school, I have liked Mark's gospel the best. The pupils were an interesting group, mainly girls, several from Greek Cypriot families, some Christians and some agnostics, most with little idea about even who St Paul was. Together we studied the gospels, tried to see what gave them their individual character, noted how Matthew and Luke had used Mark as their basic source, asked what their particular purpose was. In fact, one year, instead of giving addresses at the Good Friday three-hour meditation, I read the whole of Mark's gospel, and asked the class along, because from start to finish it is the story of the Passion of Jesus Christ, and I wanted them to hear it for themselves.

We also learnt, in the words of that time-honoured phrase 'most scholars agree', that Mark has no record of the resurrection appearances. The twelve verses that appear in small italic print in your Bibles after chapter 16.8 were added later to make up for what was thought to be a deficiency. So the gospel actually ends with the words:

> And they [the women] went out and fled from the tomb;
> for trembling and astonishment had come upon them;
> and they said nothing to any one, for they were afraid.

For an evangelist telling the good news of God's love this seems an odd note on which to end, for they were afraid. Yet I believe it is vital for Christians not to separate out the crucifixion and resurrection into separate categories, but to discover the power of the resurrection within the crucifixion itself. And as I hope will become plain, Mark has managed to do this with great effect. It takes us back to the discussion about the Negro spiritual 'Were you there when they crucified my Lord?' and its haunting refrain 'Sometimes it causes me to tremble, tremble, tremble'.

In 1917 a German theologian, Rudolf Otto, published a great book called *The Idea of the Holy* in which he tries to explain that strange feeling that we sometimes have of being confronted by the holiness of God. He says that we meet holiness through a feeling of 'mysterium tremendum'. Simply to translate those words as 'tremendous mystery' doesn't do them justice. It would be more accurate to talk of a 'mysterious tremor' which comes upon us and as it were shakes our whole being. Otto suggests that this 'mysterium tremendum' is what the Bible calls the 'fear of the Lord', and he describes the meaning of fear in this context as it is captured in a phrase like, 'and he stood aghast'.

Or, yet again, we might speak of 'religious dread', a dread that stirs in us the feeling of something uncanny, eerie or weird. He writes:

> The awe or dread may indeed be so overwhelmingly great
> that it seems to penetrate the very marrow, making a
> man's hair bristle and his limbs quake. But it may also
> steal upon him almost unobserved as the gentlest of
> agitations, a mere fleeting shadow passing across his
> mood.

This sounds to me like a very good account both of the religious experience of the women at the tomb – trembling, and astonishment had come upon them – and of the refrain, 'Sometimes it causes me to tremble, tremble, tremble'. Otto also speaks of what he calls the 'involuntary shudder', which he identifies as a very primitive response to religious experience, to the recognition of God, and which still has an important part to play in present-day Christian response. He says that the soul is ennobled beyond measure where it trembles inwardly to the farthest fibre of its being; and that the shudder is expressed within Christian worship in the words of the Sanctus: Holy, Holy, Holy, Lord God Almighty.

In a moment I would like to give what I believe to be contemporary examples of the 'mysterium tremendum', but first there is one other point that Otto makes which I think helps us to see what St Mark was getting at. He says that under the influence of the 'mysterium tremendum' 'there is a feeling of one's own submergence, of being dust and ashes and nothingness'. And this encounter with God forms the raw material for the feeling of religious humility. Now, where in Mark's picture of Jesus does the new life of the Kingdom of God begin? Answer: immediately after Peter has identified Jesus as the Christ, the Messiah, at Caesarea Philippi, when Jesus teaches them that this path to glory will involve suffering: for whoever would save his life will lose it, and whoever will lose his life for my sake and the gospel's, the same will save it. Here is the secret of the resurrection life, if only you can see it. What need have we of knock-down proofs, of stories of resurrection appearances, when eternal life itself is staring us in the face?

I believe that British Christians in our comparatively pain-free, tolerant, happy-go-lucky society have played down the sense of the 'mysterium tremendum' and replaced it with a soft-centred religion that either jollies us along or lulls us to sleep. That is probably why it is less attractive to people. But there are experiences which bring us into head-on collision with the ultimacy of God, experiences that can make the language of Thomas Cranmer's 'Prayer of Humble Access' or 'General Confession' relevant again: We are not worthy so much as to gather up the crumbs under thy table; the remembrance of our sins is grievous into us, the burden of them is intolerable.

Personally, I often find the 'mysterium tremendum' through the frontier-breaking vision of art, but that may be because my life so far has been insulated from tragedy and great crisis. Your own stories no doubt would be different. So what fills me with that religious shudder?

The power of a great building, like when in D. H. Lawrence's *The Rainbow*, Will Brangwen feels his soul soar into the lofty spaces of Lincoln Cathedral. I imagine that great church buildings have this effect when they manage to symbolise the infinite space of the universe, and our finite smallness within it, and at the same time to proclaim the faith that God values each one of us uniquely.

Or when I was watching a television production of *Twelfth Night* recently, I found myself spitefully joining in the baiting and mocking of Malvolio until the poor man is completely broken and he cries:

> 'Why have you suffer'd me to be imprison'd,
> Kept in a dark house, visited by a priest,
> And made the most notorious geck and gull
> That e'er invention play'd on? Tell me why.'

As he spoke those words I recognise in myself that killer instinct of the baying packhound that I spoke of earlier, and it makes me shudder. It is like a revelation of the importance of disinterested compassion, fellow-feeling, call it what you like – a revelation that sadly is often missed in the day-to-day images of starvation, cruelty and social alienation. I see beyond prejudice – he deserved it, he's a wimp, he has a poisonous ego – to the love which redeems life.

But it is the effect of music, in all its non-verbal power, that for many of us brings us into the mysterious and exciting domain of revelation.

One of the great descriptions of a 'mysterium tremendum' experience is in Shaffer's play *Amadeus* – it works magnificently on stage, and almost equally well in the stage directions. Salieri, Mozart's rival, is looking with admiration at some of Mozart's original scores and wishing that he had the talent to write music like this. (Remember that shameful desire to see the mighty fallen!) He says, 'I was staring through the cage of those meticulous ink strokes at an Absolute Beauty'.

Then the stage directions continue – and it is unusual for the stage directions to compete with the text itself for poetic power –

> (And out of the thundering roar writhes and rises the
> clear sound of a soprano, singing the Kyrie from the C
> Minor Mass. The accretion of noise around her voice
> falls away – it is suddenly clear and bright – then clearer
> and brighter. The light also grows bright: too bright:

burning white then scalding white. Salieri rises in the
downpour of the music which is growing even louder –
filling the theatre – as the soprano yields to the full
chorus, fortissimo, singing its massive counterpoint.
This is the loudest sound the audience has yet heard.
Salieri staggers towards us, holding the manuscripts in
his hand, like a man caught in a tumbling and violent
sea. Finally the drums crash in below. Salieri drops the
portfolio of manuscripts – and falls senseless to the
ground. At the same second the music explodes into a
long, echoing distorted boom, signifying some dreadful
annihilation.)

Shaffer plays on the pun of Mozart's name, Amadeus – loved
by God. Why does God love this vulgar little man and give
him such genius? And, without turning a comparison into
disrespect, I find it helpful to think of Jesus as the Divine
Artist, loved by God, and able to draw out in me that sense
of wondering dread.

There is a line from the Book of Ecclesiasticus favoured
by headmasters, 'The fear of the Lord is the beginning of
wisdom' (Sirach 1.14). In its context it provides a link
between the right response  to the crucifixion and an understanding of the resurrection: 'The fear of the Lord is glory
and exultation, and gladness, and a crown of rejoicing. The
fear of the Lord delights the heart, and gives gladness and
long life. With him who fears the Lord it will go well at the
end: on the day of his death he will be blessed' (Sirach
1.11–13). In other words, fear of God does not leave us full
of despair and pessimism, but opens the way to happiness
and life.

Some of you may find this emphasis on fear unhelpful.
Surely the whole purpose of the Passion is to take away our
fears and give us assurance of God's saving love and kindness. As the first letter of John says, 'There is no fear in
love, for perfect love casts out fear'. But we are not talking
about fear as in being frightened of one who we think is out
to hurt us. That certainly is cast out by God's love. But I
am equally sure that no Christian should be happy with a
cuddly God, whose principal purpose is to give comfort, like
one of those soft, shimmery objects that some people keep
in their pockets to calm them down when they are feeling
tense. If your God is a cuddly God, then your religion

deserves the taunt of my student critic that religion is no more than an emotional crutch.

No, the fear at the end of Mark's gospel is a shudder of genuine awe that the body they had come to anoint has gone, and also a bewildered fear – what do we do now? Something is being demanded of us. As Morna Hooker says in her splendid book *The Meaning of Mark*: 'How typical of the Markan Jesus that [the angel's] message is: Go and you will see him. Not: you will see him and then you must go. The message demands a response.' Just as in the healing of the man with the withered hand, where Jesus said to the man, stretch out your hand. How was he to stretch it out? A response was demanded. He stretched forth his arm by faith. And so the crucifixion demands a response from us, unless we are totally insensitive to what was going on. Sometimes it causes me to tremble, tremble, tremble. It is as if Mark were saying to us at the end of his story: look, if you haven't got the message by now you never will. You wouldn't believe even if one were to rise from the dead. But, if you have understood the teaching of Jesus the Messiah when he said, Anyone who would be my disciple must take up his cross and follow me, then you have got the point, and through your faith the resurrection must necessarily follow, because the beginning of discipleship is the beginning of life.

Let me conclude this personal exposition of the Passion by trying to illustrate the resurrection from an experience that I hope is common to all of us. Each one of us will know someone, or a small number of people, whom we truly admire and respect, and to whom we turn for advice. In my experience such people have been the ones who, apart from having obvious gifts, have accepted me for what I am, and perhaps have surprised me by their acceptance. I have wanted to live up to their expectations of me precisely because they have accepted me. I could not bear to let them down. That would be a form of betrayal. So their acceptance has been like a judgement upon me. If they had been different – gifted, but pompous, destructively critical – I should probably have responded with reckless aggression, in self-defence. But their acceptance has not left me with that escape route. Graciousness has to be responded to with graciousness, however much it hurts my pride. Therefore, I have feared those people because of their acceptance, feared really the possibility of my own disloyalty, my own failure, that I might let them down. It is the same with God. It is the same with our Lord Jesus Christ. With God my fear is of my own sin, because he accepts me as I am, and I know he loves me as I am, he wants me to prosper, and I am afraid that I will let him down. This loyalty to him grows all the stronger when I see the pain and torture he is willing to bear because of his love for me. For greater love has no man than this, that a man should lay down his life for a friend.

I want to say a resounding 'Yes' to the one who I know is tremendous in his power and goodness. I want to say yes to the one who is willing to empty himself of this power for me. I want to say yes to the one who, at the same time, accepts me and does me the honour of challenging me to follow in his footsteps.

# Mass for Three Voices

INTROIT

It may seem odd to start with feet, but feet is an obvious
way into this story.

Easter fell early and was accompanied by sharp frosts
that necessitated the lighting of the paraffin lamps in the
greenhouse at about six o'clock in the evening. On Maundy
Thursday we were wrapped up like carol singers when we
walked to a neighbouring church for an ecumenical celebration of the institution of the Last Supper. Inside we were
grateful for our scarves and overcoats, as the caretaker had
forgotten to turn on the heating – it being an irregular
service. At the gospel the curate had decided to enact the
story of the washing of the disciples' feet, which in the pages
of the New Testament is a narrative of peculiarly dignified
and emotive power. For the purpose he had invited a group
of men and women to be the recipients of this mark of
Christ's self-effacing service and hospitality. At the appropriate moment they stepped forward barefoot and took their
places on chairs either side of the altar. Instead of being dry
and dusty, their tacky feet left damp imprints on the marble.
One man shivered in his shirt sleeves, another rolled up his
trouser legs like an Englishman paddling at the seaside, and
as the curate, robed in white and carrying a towel, dabbed
the feet of the first woman, she struggled to hold down her
skirt so that we shouldn't see the pearly flesh above her
knees. I had to bite my tongue and think of marmalade
pudding to stop myself giggling at the wholly ludicrous sight
of all these white and cornigerous feet, piously and self-
consciously offered in the service of the liturgy. At that
moment I realised what had always been true, that I had
no desire to be a chiropodist.

Symbolism and metaphor can only work effectively if

78

they are contextually right, which is another way of saying that the image and the idea it portrays must easily connect. Not that the image needs to be a commonplace, because in many ways the more startling and original it is, the more revealing it becomes. But whether the image is startling or ordinary it is essential that the reader or hearer should be able to locate it in his experience. For example, it is no use trying to spend money in a society that bases its commerce on barter. Your tarnished coins merely insult the tradesman, who has no way of understanding their value, and he would much rather have bright beads instead.

But bread, wine and olive oil are the real symbols of my story, and I shall locate them where they most truly belong, and most eloquently speak, in the warmth of summer in Italy, in that leg and foot of land which wades across the Mediterranean Sea, whose empire once stretched to Judaea where these staples of life were to be given a meaning that would change the world.

## THE STORY

My friend Leandro is a hunter, countryman and school-teacher. We first met when he and his wife, Teresa, stayed in our house as paying guests in North London. They had brought a party of Italian schoolchildren to learn English, and we needed money for our summer holiday. I knew he was a hunter from the moment he stood in the garden and lifted his arms as if aiming a gun at the thrushes and black-birds that grubbed and fluttered around the herbaceous border. But we were shy with each other, meeting at meal times, otherwise going our own ways. Besides, our relation-ship was strictly a business arrangement – bed, breakfast and evening meal – and (it clearly unnerved him) he was living in the house of a priest, and a married one at that. I was perfectly happy to keep our two guests at arm's length, and it would have remained that way had it not been for the vegetables. Well, that's not entirely true – my wife is the very daughter of prodigality when it comes to hospitality. Anyway, each evening I would come home from the allot-ment with my bike basket packed with lettuce, peas, new potatoes, strawberries and raspberries (*lamponi* in Italian – little lanterns). Eating home-grown food together was deeply meaningful to Leandro, a sign of the fellowship of nature, and in return he began to produce from his room bottles of country wine and grappa that he had distilled himself, in his garage at home. He asked to see the allotment, learn the English names of plants, explore the countryside, see the habitat of the pheasant, the partridge and the hare.

Last time we were in Falconara, Leandro had arranged with farming friends from the foothills of the Apennines a peasant hunter's feast. It was out of season, so the pheasants came from the deep freeze, but the fish he had caught early that morning in the shallow blue haze of the Adriatic. You really ought to see Leandro as he stern-paddles his flat-bottomed boat, all creaky and sturdy and proud-prowed, away from the beach. He is a wood-block man, made of two square boxes, one upon the other. The weight of his square torso sways with the oar; his massive calves scarcely incline beneath the baggy khaki shorts that reach below the knees. Bare-chested, he looks straight ahead with sea sparkle in his face, and across his belly a fierce scar burns, like a prophetic parable, where, at the age of four, he had swallowed a Fascist badge of Mussolini which had to be gouged out with a knife.

# KYRIE

Part of the excitement of preparing to go on holiday is deciding what to read. I like to achieve a mixture of escape, sense of place, and something a bit mind-stretching. Escape, because holidays are meant to help you get out of yourself; place, because there is a kind of jarring dislocation in lying on a hot Italian beach reading about, say, the rural England of the nineteenth-century novel; and thought, because I shall almost certainly have to preach my next sermon out of the ideas gleaned while away. Last year I sought the advice of an English don, shot her some line about exploring the Italian mind, anthropology of the culture, and she almost took my pretension seriously. Well, let me see, there's Umberto Eco, *The Name of the Rose*. Or (sudden breathy enthusiasm) what about Silone? Yes, Ignazio Silone. He's worth reading. Try *Vino e Pane*. Or, what's the other one? *Fontamara*. At the time I wasn't thinking of writing about bread and wine, and *Fontamara* sounded more romantic, more Italian, less theological. Then, as I began to read, my mind began to boggle! Incredibly powerful stuff! Sit down you swaggering bronzed Adonises, keep still you coquetting signorinas and listen to this. What do you know about your country? What do you know about the Fascists and how they swindled the peasants of the village of Fontamara in Abruzzo, drove them to despair, and futile revolt, by calculated and merciless exploitation? What do you know and what do you care?

But the Adonises and coquettes refuse to sit down. They pose and spoon like flamingos, ankle-deep in the tepid Adriatic, self-attentive, skin-conscious. The summer, even here, is too short for philosophy. While in 1930s Fontamara corruption spreads like rust through nails left out in the rain. Even the priest succumbs. Even the priest. You are not surprised. And have things changed? When the peasants ask for a mass to be said in their village the greasy Don Abbacchio doubles the price, making a swindle out of the grace of Christ. But they scrape the money together for the sacrament, and the priest comes.

> The only really beautiful thing in the church was the
> picture of the eucharist on the altar. Jesus, with a piece
> of white bread in his hand, was saying: This is my body,
> white bread is my body, white bread is the Son of God,
> white bread is truth and life. Jesus was not taking the
> maize bread that cafoni eat, or the tasteless substitute
> for bread that is the consecrated wafer of the priests.
> Jesus had in his hand a piece of real white bread and
> was saying: This (white bread) is my body, which is
> truth and life. What he meant was that he who has
> white bread has Me (God). He who does not have white
> bread, who has only maize bread, is outside the grace
> of God, does not know the truth, has no life. He lives
> on garbage, like pigs and donkeys, and goats.

The injustice which raged in the hearts of the peasants was that they must work in the sweat of their brow to grow the wheat which makes the white bread, but they never get to eat it, because they are too poor and can only afford maize bread. And here is Jesus holding up white bread as his gift to all people.

## GLORIA

The fat priest who piggy-backed through life on the stooped shoulders of the peasants preached to them that day about acrobatics. About the merit of contorting oneself for God. To be exact he told the story of Giuseppe da Copertino, a popular local saint, holy but illiterate, who had taken the vows of poverty, chastity and obedience. But Giuseppe could not read Latin, so when the other monks were saying the divine office he did somersaults instead. Imagine the sober brothers leaning back on their misericords chanting the psalms in religious monotone, while Giuseppe, wild and free, springs, leaps and vaults over the flagstones of the nave. Listen to the rhythm of his praise: the pah, pah, pah, pah of the quick succession of his somersaults; the padding syncopation of his cartwheels; acceleration, silence, then the smack of leather on stone as he runs up, spins through the air, and lands, pulling his body to elegant attention, spreading his arms in a graceful gesture of acknowledgement. He bows. This is liberation theology, a new movement in theology. Let us all praise God with our talents. O be joyful in the Lord all ye clowns, jugglers, and fools of Christ, for your exuberance lifts even the Spirit of God. How do I know? How do you think? The Blessed Virgin Mary bestowed upon Giuseppe the gift of levitation so that he was able to cavort and tumble up the pillars, across the clerestory windows, into the spaces of the vaulted ceiling. His soul leapt up to his God in a Te Deum of movement, in a Gloria in Excelsis of surreal agility, muscle and sinew, breath and perspiration, praising God in the heights, while his brothers below on their knees or perched on their misericords antiphoned to one another across the choir their litany of dutiful Latin.

When Giuseppe got to heaven he was made welcome beyond all his hopes. God said to him, what would you like, Giuseppe – you can choose anything you like. Are you sure? he says. Do you really mean I can choose anything? The humble monk searched his soul to see whether he actually dare ask God for so great a gift. What I would really like, he said, is a big piece of white bread.

## OFFERTORY

That same morning Leandro had asked me to fetch the bread for the feast from a village in the hills. Creamy, bubbly, white bread that was baked in a wood-heated cloam oven which stood at the side of the road in the village centre. The oven belonged to the commune, or local authority and, when it wasn't being used by the shop, was available to any villager for family baking. All you had to do was take your faggots and logs, light a fire inside the oven, and when the bricks glowed white, rake out the embers; then it was ready to bake. The whole structure, built in concrete, was the size of a bus shelter, like the cockpit of a motor cruiser inside, with bench seats around the open end, and the oven where the cabin doors would be. The uncooked loaves, yellow white moons, bulging with their own fermenting density, were slipped across the oven floor on a long-handled wooden paddle, deftly manipulated by a woman in a black, but flour-drenched frock. As she worked you could see the domed roof of the hot cavity perfectly constructed in brick, the shape of a pine cone. She said she was baking for her family; not just two or three loaves, but a couple of dozen, each weighing about a kilo. As she packed the oven she talked. Each loaf that entered was a prayer for the one who would eat it: the daughter-in-law who had just had a baby; the boy who was working in the paper mill at Fabriano – what might the silly goose be breathing into his lungs? Another son had left his wife two years to the day after the wedding. How could it possibly be his fault, he was so handsome and so gentle? Who was going to feed him now if it wasn't his Mama? All her maternal and grandmaternal cares and anxieties were contained in those loaves which she had lovingly prepared and now offered in the furnace as an oblation to the god of family solidarity and better times.

People stood around and chatted, like they do in parables, as if gathered at the well or in the market place, discussing work, the price of shoes, and the farmer who had been crushed to death under a vineyard tractor (one of those specially designed for the narrow rows between the vines), which toppled over on a steep corner. The community was gathered and symbolised in the bread of the cloam oven which they all shared.

# THE STORY

We set out for the rustic dinner one hot July afternoon, with the roof of the yellow 2CV rolled back as far as it would go. In our car were Leandro, Alfonso, Angelo and me – all boys together. Alfonso, Leandro's cousin, is semi-retired now. Never having married, he lives *in famiglia* in Leandro's household, unobtrusively, undemanding, occasionally doing part-time work in a local hotel. Angelo is bigger, less sensitive than Alfonso, a potman and general odd-job man with big goalkeeper's hands tough and dirt-cracked. This is the first time that I have met him and our initial exchange of glances and his bearing tells of a man who has hardened himself against feeling, and today is, to say the least, equivocal about this foreign priest who has been admitted to the brotherhood. As we come down the hill they jabber and chortle while I, cubicled off by incomprehension, gaze out across the kerosene shimmer of Falconara airport which lies in the flood-plain of the river Esino.

– What are they talking about? I ask Leandro, whose English is good.

– They discuss a bad woman that is in the hotel . . . you understand. And she does not pay the padrone. There are many people in the bar. So he whistles his dog. His dog pulls the garments from her bag. The garments are made of leather. The dog is so passionate he eats the garments.

Alfonso and Angelo are leaning forward in the back seats, eager to see how the priest will react. When I laugh, they scream and nod and clap their hands, affirmed in the ordinary salacious talk of life while I am contemplating the meaning of pilgrimage, or something like it. I expect they are right.

I should have told you, although I am not certain how important it is, that Leandro's charisma and his eccentricity (he actually models himself on his hero Duke Federico of Urbino, the one with the great angular profile and red pillar-box hat) both stem from his love of what he calls 'the old Italian way'. This has to do with the bonds of kinship and friendship, living in an extended family, being recklessly hospitable, eating plenty of herbs, and the Roman handshake, which is hard to describe, except that you clasp each other's thumb rather in the manner of arm wrestling. This is a big symbol of commitment, like sealing your relationship in blood.

Then we turn inland and up the long valley. Leandro drives at a constant 50 kilometres per hour, sounding his horn in a raucous continuo against the modern drivers who indicate with fists, headlights, and a gesture meaning 'you cuckold', that he is holding up progress. We are a lot of cranks pretending that we can live by the old ways and the old rural customs. And why not? Across the valley to the north the medieval ramparts of Jesi rise out of the plain and seem to float on time itself. They absorb modernity with the same miraculous capacity that the sea absorbs tons of carbon dioxide. We have a continuity with the past which is more than nostalgia. It is to do with values and radicalism, respect for our roots, honouring our father and mother, the contentment of knowing what is enough.

Now we turn left to climb the spur to the side of the valley, along the road that leads to Cupramontana, a hilltop town where for a day each October the new wine flows freely from a tap in the wall of the town hall, like Midas' fountain of sweet wine from which the satyrs drank, or as if Moses had cleft the rock of the building with his rod. Immediately the terrain changes. In place of the lowland corn stubble and galaxies of sunflowers, the humped fields, striped with the latticework of vines, swell and trough around us. These are the vines of the Verdicchio grape which produce one of the best-known white wines of Italy, straw-green and 'versatile', as it says in the tourist blurb. The temperature has hardly dropped since one o'clock. The hills and sky merge into a haze of olive smoke, and as we drive through the villages people hide in corners of coolness, behind curtains and in shadows. In the car the men are sweaty.

## SANCTUS

Holy, holy, holy, the three voices sing this music weaving a polyphony of worship, three wavy lines across a screen, heartbeats, lifelines, threading melody with melody and rhythms of the seasons. Music made from the counterpoint of questions. Questions sharpened by their interrelation. Three imitative themes displaying degrees of kinship: the tenor speaks, the alto answers, their dissonance resolves as the treble enters, all edging towards God and touching the hem of his divine mystery.

Christian theology begins with two people at the street corner discussing the price of bread; or with oil and wine poured into a wound by a good Samaritan. The question is how can distant holiness be caught in simple rude necessities? Suppose the baker of the bread were an angry, red-faced man who liked to commit adultery; could God gladly enter that corrupt loaf? Perhaps that is why so many churches use wafers baked by holy nuns. Or does the incarnation mean that all things are suffused with his mysterious holiness just waiting to be transformed by faith? Holy is the prostitute's bag, holy are the dirt-cracked hands, holy the acrobatic priest.

But reflect on this. It is not the bread that changes, it is the one who eats it; not the bread, but the person, who is made holy. Let's face it, I do not find this genuflection easy – I am not one to grovel or crouch – yet kneeling before the sacrament in humble awe you open yourself to moments of holy transformation.

I have just read a poem by Anne Ridler called 'A Taste for Truth' which makes the point with sensitive insight.

> For *miracle*, they say, translate *a sign*.
> If God made water into wine
> What was his meaning? That his laws
> Are not immutable? Though our state is miserable
> Yet all might live in glory if they chose?
> Wine of our joy and water of our tears
> Are not so incompatible as we think
> If the atoms did not change, but those who drank.

## THANKSGIVING

At the farm the fish were to be grilled on the embers of a fire made from last year's vine cuttings in the untidy farm-yard. Here hens scavenged and a tethered dog tried to escape its circular territory, full of absurd canine joy as it jumped and leapt hopefully at human contact. Under an orchard of apple and peach trees, behind the bars of a shelter that resembled a wartime dug-out in the hillside, grunted a sow with her young, too hot to realise or care that they were to become next year's *prosciutto*. Further up the hill, behind the house, I could hear an occasional plaintive yelp, a cry really, that no one seemed to notice. I left the party to look for myself. On a mound, chained beside a small kennel, was a piebald dog like a pointer. It certainly had the broad skull and short bristly hair of that breed, but his ribcage and pelvic girdle protruded as if the bones were wearing away the skin. He pulled himself up and smiled in benign, well-tempered greeting. Why? When I stroked his head and back he was grateful, and I felt I must continue to touch him from compassion even though the bristles of his coat fell out like dead needles from a Christmas tree and there were sores along his vertebrae. Why? I discovered the reason. Truffles. He was used for sniffing out truffles, the tuber which grows in the oak forests of the mountains, and is so highly valued for its taste and aroma. Basically, the dog had been conditioned to a Pavlovian programme which states: food is always the result of finding truffles. If the dog is not kept hungry that essential bit of software will get wiped off the disk. What credit to the dog that he greeted me with such equilibrium, like a gentle martyr. My protests were explicit, but only as far as I dare go within the terms of my contract as honoured guest, but I was offended at this old Italian way, and felt that the fellowship of nature, which must be between man and animal as well as man and man, had been broken.

Leandro had brought the meat, and I had brought the bread, so the farmer provided the wine. Nadino led us into his medieval *cantina*, a small chapel, long since abandoned as a place of worship, now half buried underground, cool as a catacomb, in which stood in place of altar, font and stations of the cross a wine press and five vast oak casks, like dark echoing rooms, waiting for the juice of the new vintage. The wine we were to drink was in demijohns, giant jars randomly placed on tables, shelves and the earthen floor of the winery. Deftly Nadino took a length of rubber tube, inserted one end into the demijohn, sucked the other with his mouth, spat, and then the liquid came flowing through into the beakers on the bench. It was cool and aromatic. As we raised our glasses the efficacy of the ceremony created a sort of numinous feel in the old church. *Buono, buono. Molto buono. Buonissimo*, said everyone in appreciation to the host. Nadino accepted the praise with a modest toss of the head as if to say, *Di niente*, it is nothing, don't mention it. Probably the wine was very ordinary, but as the result of this small miracle it tasted like a *premier cru* of the finest vintage because we were in touch with its origins, the vines, the vats, the vigneron, the sun, the olive smoke haze, the necessities of nature, like a medieval tapestry of bright colours, red and gold and green.

Outside, in the shade of the farmhouse was a rustic table and a variety of stools and seats, including a torn canvas director's chair, in which Leandro sat. The meats were on a common plate. The signora, Nadino's wife, had collected a fresh salad. We had watched her walking up between the vines, bow-legged but athletic, in a simple frock, and frayed straw hat, with her salad basket over her arm. There was an inventive laughter in her work-tough frame and gappy smile and the creasing of her leathery skin.

Then Angelo took the bread in his dirt-cracked hands and broke it over the edge of the table, unaffectedly, easily, and passed a piece to everyone, instinctively, not politely or ingratiatingly, but natural, as natural as eating his own food. He didn't know it, perhaps none of them saw it, but I was moved. It made me emotional and grateful this simple act. And seeing the fish and the bread like this, I thought of the Feeding of the Five Thousand. Here was a simplicity and communality enforced by the sun, in which we celebrated life in the Mediterranean basics of bread, oil, wine and fish. I saw Christ in that attentive, unexpected act of dirty-fingered Angelo breaking the loaf over the unscrubbed table – Angelo, who an hour before had sniggered and bawdied over the tale of the prostitute's clothes.

## BENEDICTUS

Much banging of the table.

– I propose to make a toast, shouts Leandro. How do you say? Bottoms up! Here's mud in the eye! I make a toast to the bread, oil and wine, the elements of our Mediterranean way. First the bread which feeds us and gives us good company. *Con pane*, company – the Italian way. Second the Verdicchio, the Verdicchio of Nadino, which gladdens the heart. And third, oil, the most difficult word in English for the

Italian student. Oil, ill, I'll, eel, heal, hill, heel. What a language!

Leandro pronounces oil with a slight aspiration so that it sounds like h'oil.

Yes, the oil of the olive, which Jacob poured as an oblation over the stone pillar he had erected to mark the holy place where he dreamt of angels ascending and descending on a ladder. The olive which Greek mythology claims to have been created by the goddess Athena in her struggle with Poseidon over the patronage of Athens. *Olea europaea*, cultivated from the wild olive, indigenous to the eastern Mediterranean, whose golden, green juice was taken in a ram's horn by Zadok the priest to anoint the breast of the son of David before the crowd in acclamation shouted 'Long live King Solomon'. Your social status could be gauged by the oiliness of your sauce, so crucial was the olive to the economy of the ancient world – you could even use it as a currency. Indeed, you feared to be without it lest your bread be dry and insipid, as we see from the widow who contemplated death until Elijah blessed her with a cruse that constantly replenished itself. In the Garden of Gethsemane, gnarled into shapes that seem to live, the olive trees were the witnesses of Christ's torment of spirit, of his struggle of conscience and will against his calling to suffering and self-sacrifice. He was betrayed beneath the olive trees, but despite the blackness of *olea sativa*, the olive is not a fruit of darkness but of light – the wise virgins came to the marriage feast, the heavenly banquet, with lamps burning and oil a-plenty to light heaven itself until Christ the bridegroom should appear.

That 'oil' and 'heal' and 'whole' should share such an assonance in our language is one of the happy accidents of art, because the soothing, medicinal effect of the olive has long been recognised, by for instance the Good Samaritan who poured oil and wine into the lacerations of the unfortunate traveller on the Road to Jericho. Still today the Mediterranean peasant uses oil as a cure-all, and takes it as a prophylactic, hoping to find the secret of eternal life which the olive is thought to possess.

I tell you all this about the humble olive, which can be eaten stuffed with meat in Ascoli, or with pimento at English parties, in order that you might begin to understand why it became the mark of kings, the sign of the Spirit in baptism, and the symbol of healing in unction. It is the oil of life, the essence of nourishment, health and righteousness, of light, goodness and prosperity. These are the gifts a good king could bring upon his nation.

## AGNUS DEI

But this is symbolic talk. We must get the symbols in their place or they become as misleading as a misplaced road sign. Symbols are not absolutes, they are miniature stories that ask questions rather than define answers. Christian symbols confront us with God, and travel across boundaries – that is their purpose. How can we celebrate a universal faith in imagery of abundant food when millions of people in the world die from starvation? The difficulty is often raised as part of the more general, yet naggingly precise, question, why does a loving and powerful God allow suffering in the world? Surely the poetic sentiments of Psalm 104, for example, are just wishful thinking: 'Thou dost cause the grass to grow for the cattle, and plants for man to cultivate, that he may bring forth food from the earth, and wine to gladden the heart of man, oil to make his face shine, and bread to strengthen man's heart'. It's not true. It's not true that God our maker provides for all our wants to be supplied. We can prove it, easily; take the futility of just one small baby sucking at her mother's shrivelled breast. There are great swathes of the earth's surface quite inimical to the growing of crops: the Arctic regions, the deserts – a quarter of the earth's surface, in fact. In the Third World the population explodes where food is scarce and farming methods primitive. How many people know extreme deprivation and crippling hunger? Yet the central symbol of Christian worship is bread and wine.

Ah, yes, but don't forget what the bread and wine symbolise: one hanging on a cross who in his agony cries out, 'I thirst'.

Neither do you solve the moral problem of starvation by wishing it on everyone, or not daring to talk about food for fear of causing offence. When he addressed the poor Jesus didn't think it odd to speak of the Kingdom of Heaven as a great feast, a wedding banquet, a dinner provided in the master's hall to which people from the highways and byways were pressed to come in. He made their mouths water. You solve the problem of starvation by a more just distribution of food. The imagery of bread and wine might pose the question, why starvation, just as the imagery of the lion lying down with the lamb poses the question, why violence? but the answer is not to be found in neat ethical or political dogma, it is to be found inside you, where the bread and wine is to be absorbed. The image confronts you.

The cornucopian poetry of the Old Testament itself needs to be put into context. Do you suppose that the people who wrote this stuff had never experienced hunger, plague, famine, or the devastation of their crops by pests? Had they not laboriously dragged the rocks and stones that blunted the plough to the middle of their small hard fields, and then observed with resignation the fading strength of the corn under the relentless heat of the sun? Had they not themselves questioned God's inconsistency and asked why he allowed hunger and disease? But they believed, as in the story of Joseph in Egypt, that faithfulness to their God brought its reward. Above all they saw God's creative nature and ultimate purpose of salvation symbolised in a picture of plenty, of the desert springing to life, and vines and figs dripping with fruit. They were not making a false or sentimental claim that everything in God's garden was lovely when it was not. The images of plenty were like voices crying in the wilderness, visions of home dreamt about in exile, or signs of hope in adversity. The irrepressible optimism of the Jews is their greatest gift to religion, a hope that is defiant, irrational, and grounded in a picture of the creative love of God. This was the root of the messianic hope, the Jews' great gift to Christianity. And Jesus came into Galilee proclaiming the new age and quoting from Isaiah, 'The Spirit of the Lord is upon me, because he has anointed me with oil'. The age of the banquet has come, of healing and liberty and comforting. 'As a garden causes what is sown to spring up, so the Lord will cause righteousness and praise to spring forth before the nations.' The age of bread and wine.

## THE HOMILY

My dear friends, how are memories made? What causes the chemistry of our minds to print a stronger code for one experience than another, or distinguish between revelation and commonplace? This hillside barbecue, with its cast of rustic players, whose speech I barely understand, often comes back to me now as a gospel narrative brought to life in my own experience, its symbolic power all the greater for the inevitable subordination of words to gesture.

How much has the stylisation of the eucharist over the centuries distanced the central act of Christian worship from the occasions when the disciples ate with their Lord, on a hillside, or at a wedding reception, in the house of Zacchaeus, with the women at Bethany, in the upper room at Passover, at Emmaus, or eating fish for breakfast on the Galilean beach? Nothing formal, except for the ordinary formalities of hospitality and giving thanks to God, the sort of thing every good Jew would do, yet occasions of transformation when, to borrow a phrase, water was turned to wine. The fact that it was at a meal laden with all the gravity of the anticipation of his death that Jesus said 'Do this in remembrance of me' should not blind us to the truth that the eucharist is also a feast of the resurrection, and should therefore draw its imagery just as much from the meal at Emmaus, or the feasting and dancing at the return of the Prodigal Son, best robe, fatted calf, and all.

I invite you to look at the gospels and there you will find a Jesus who was not fussed about ritual, for example sabbath observance and ritual washing, so long as a person could discover all the delight and excitement of knowing God. The resurrection has just the same uncluttered freshness as Jesus had in his ministry. The resurrection takes those who experience it by surprise, in locked rooms, on the Damascus Road, five hundred people at once. And in our own time people will describe their sudden awareness of the risen Lord in unpredictable and seemingly inappropriate places; in remote and isolated parts of the world, in prison, through relationships, in nightclubs, in the Stock Exchange, in sickness. Christ is not concerned about being appropriate, or conventional, or observing protocol, because the resurrection has broken loose from that in us which is self-conscious, cautious, fussy, legalistic and restrictive. God shows us his freedom, freedom like that of the Spirit to blow where it wills.

So in life together and in worship Christians must risk God's freedom. At the eucharist, why should not the children, even the very young children, eat bread with their parents? Perhaps that point would be more obvious if bread like Angelo's loaf were used instead of the very stylised wafers, often with an image of the crucified Christ impressed upon them. If the eucharist is a common meal prefiguring the heavenly banquet, then shall children be excluded from it, as if both food and God were only for grown-ups? Or is it too holy for them to touch? It is not the bread that changes, but those who eat it who are changed.

Or if a group of Christians are together in a house and they want to break bread together and use the words of St Paul's account of the Last Supper, why not? Does it matter that a priest is not present? Where two or three are gathered together in my name, there am I in the midst of them. Jesus doesn't say: Do this in remembrance of me, but only if a priest is present. Jesus didn't invent the priesthood. Let's start running some of the risks of the resurrection, because God risks everything for men and women in his incarnation.

Yes, yes, I know. Risk-taking sounds better rhetorically than it feels in practice. The radical step, if taken unilaterally, raises questions about loyalty to the Church, solidarity with the party, and has implications for Church unity. Much better together. I respect that point of view. Yet the Church worldwide is a very fragmented society, and individual churches are often very cumbersome organisations, in which it is often the case that prophetic risk-taking is the only effective way forward.

Now this may surprise you. God is not so much concerned with the Church as with the world. His resurrection is not exclusively for the Church, but for the world. Remember what he said: I came not to call the righteous, but sinners to repentance. So while God comes to us in the breaking of bread, he does so surprisingly. That is to say, where we least expect him. And at a reflective level, we might ask ourselves how often we walk with Christ and fail to recognise him. Or how often do we stand between him and his revelation by smothering ourselves in prejudice and prefabricated expectations, like the notion that he is only to be found when the liturgy conforms to certain historic precedents. The Good News has to be enabled to reach inside all the secular institutions too. Jesus taught people from a boat, not a pulpit, he criticised the priest and Levite who passed by on the other side, praised the prostitute who anointed his feet, and dined with an extortionate tax-collector.

Blessed are the risk-takers for the resurrection of Christ shall be theirs.

# Mary of Magdala

When Mary of Magdala came into the garden early that morning, her vision was salt-blurred, eyes blotched and blackened with exhaustion. She had forced herself to watch the vile torture of the one she loved so much, and had hated her impotence to save him. She would have interposed her own body between his and the soldiers' nails, but she had been thrown roughly to one side and told the same thing would happen to her if she persisted. Gladly would she have been tortured with him, but she knew that it would only hurt him more.

It had all seemed to happen in slow motion. Thirty-six hours that had felt like a lifetime. A lifetime indeed, because surely now life was at an end. What future, but dreadful emptiness? She kept turning over in her mind the things he had said, the way he had changed her life, brought her out of the gutter, set her on a pedestal, to the shocked outrage of the establishment. Now in the darkness she didn't want the light to come, people would only see the ugliness of her tormented face, call her whore again. How could she face another day? She simply wanted to anoint his body and wish him rest in peace. Inwardly she smiled at the irony that when she had anointed him before, on that other occasion, with the scandalously expensive but exquisite pure nard, which caused such a rumpus, she was unwittingly anointing him for his burial.

But when she reached the tomb, the stone had been rolled away. Was there no respect for the dead? They had feared that after all he had said about rebuilding the Temple in three days, and the Son of Man coming in glory, someone might interfere with the tomb and try to make a commercial killing out of it. There was no end to human depravity. She should know.

Then when in the half-light she saw the gardener, she

didn't look at him with the loving attention that Jesus had taught her, but aggressively, thinking he might be the one who had desecrated the tomb. She was angry with him, with herself – until he spoke her name. It was the voice of acceptance, the voice of love, the voice of complete and visionary knowledge. The same tone, the same word that had once before lifted her out of self-hatred and allowed her to stand up in front of the great and the good as a person, with dignity. She wanted to fling her arms around him, kiss his face, his hands, his feet. But he prevented her.

William Temple wrote, 'Not to the Lord as he tabernacled in the flesh, subject to all the limitations of the body, is she to cling; but to the Lord in his perfect union with the Father'. What an extraordinary expression – 'tabernacled in the flesh' – even for 1940. But the great Archbishop had surely got it right: in the resurrection men and women are brought into a new relationship with God, with the eternal, with one who is immeasurably too great to be embraced by us, but whose universal love and power wraps us round and sustains us with a grace that passes understanding.

Was it an accident, do you think, that the Risen Lord appeared first to Mary of Magdala, out of whom he had cast seven devils? Perhaps after Easter, as well as in his ministry, the first people to recognise the truth about Jesus are not the educated well-to-do, nor the pillars of society, but social outcasts, sinners, simple fishermen, even the madman who lived among the tombs.

Mary was not every mother's dream of the ideal daughter. Okay. Lovely hair that she could sit on, good taste in perfume, popular, but really! What is it the psychologists say? That many girls who end up walking the streets have had loveless childhoods, been victims of childhood sexual abuse, and therefore, as soon as they are free, or perhaps before, go out in search of love. She was the archetypal converted sinner. It was right that she should be the first to meet the Risen Lord. She had already experienced the resurrection life through forgiveness, and her forgiveness depended on the extraordinary fact that a wild and unconventional rabbi, who wasn't frightened to scorn social pressure, accepted her. She had found new life, then lost it (or so it seemed) until it was confirmed to her in the garden. 'Justification by Faith is, as Paul Tillich put it, accepting the fact that we are accepted – the whole of us.' That is resurrection.

Archetypal converted sinner. Some spiritual writers describe Mary as *the* Magdalen, making her not so much a figure of history as a dramatic type, a necessary player in the drama of salvation, along with *the* Virgin and *the* Christ. One could easily add other dramatic types which symbolise aspects of human failure and aspiration, *the* Judas, *the* Pilate, *the* Rock (Peter).

She was of course a close follower of Jesus and must have grown as familiar with his teaching as the disciples themselves. In fact the argument sometimes used against the ordination of women – that Jesus did not choose any female disciples – rings a little hollow when you think of the group of women that followed him to the cross and to the grave, when the disciples had dispersed, probably in fear for their own lives.

She was a risk-taker. Being a prostitute is a risky business – the danger of disease and violence. Risk was her nature. She broke with convention in a male-dominated society and washed Jesus' feet with her own tears. In that act alone she revealed a natural talent for understanding what Jesus was driving at through his message. 'If I then, your Lord and Teacher, have washed your feet, you also ought to wash one another's feet.'

And she took the risk of love. As Jesus said of her, 'I tell you, her sins, which are many, are forgiven, for she loved much'. Sure she did, everyone knew that, as you could tell from the salacious laughter that scuttled round the room. Not exactly the kind of love that would be taken as a model for *agape*, that pure Christian, spiritual love. But she loved with a reckless prodigality. She rained love down like the petals of a cherry tree. That surely is the secret of the resurrection – to take the risk of love, to enter into the love of God with your guard down, with an eagerness that is ready to risk naivete, or appearing foolish, for the sake of the Kingdom of God.

That is why Mary of Magdala was the first person to see the Risen Lord, because she loved him with a love that left her totally bereft without him. Naturally her love was mingled with desire, but that diverting physical crush was soon forgotten when instead of seeing through a glass darkly she saw him face to face.

In his first letter to the Corinthians, St Paul speaks of all the skills, spiritual qualifications and religious observances we cite to prove that we are people of God, but insists that all of these without love are useless. Mary had that natural gift of grace. She couldn't help it. She loved without sophistication. She didn't have prophetic powers, or understand all mysteries, neither could she speak the language of the angels, she wasn't steeped in the tradition and learning of the elders, but she did have love, and therefore the resurrection came easily to her.

We, who stand looking at the resurrection, sometimes with a restlessness that borders on neurosis, can take a lesson from Mary of Magdala and approach God with a simple, loving faith. Of course we can always kid ourselves that the new life of Christ can be achieved with a certain degree of artfulness, and that he is bound to respond to our sophisticated attempts to impress, with a nice turn of phrase, a beautifully performed liturgy, a well-disciplined set of spiritual exercises. But what is really required is that we should turn to him and say to him 'Rabboni', which is to say 'Master'.

That very recognition of the lordship of Christ is the seed and kernel of the resurrection life. Jesus came that we should have life and have it abundantly. And it is such a full life that it transcends the fact of physical death, it is a light that cannot be snuffed out, a light that shines in the darkness of our despair, our failure, and our physical weakness, our pain and our sorrow, our tragedy, our pettiness, our feebleness, our sin. Day by day we die through sin, but when Jesus was lifted up he drew all men and women to himself – Mary of Magdala is a symbol of this. He wanted to re-energise a stale religion, and redeem an immoral society. His tolerance and openly generous friendship with sinners does not condone, but it redeems, and we can live with Christ, and he will live in us, as our light, our joy, and our redemption.

# Possibly a Love Story

'The impulse to worship is deep and ambiguous and old.'
Yes, Malcolm knew that. He had felt it since he didn't know
when; it ran through his cells, was printed on his genetic
map like original sin.

He was converted to Christianity at the age of thirteen
at a time when he belonged to a church youth club where
importance was attached to pinning conversion down, and
where the members exchanged embroidered stories of their
religious experience with as much bluster as they talked
about sex, except of course that St Paul warned them to
keep sex out of religion. His conversion came the September
after Dawn had found her faith at an evangelical summer
camp, much influenced by Dave, a lively curate from a
parish in Sheffield. Malcolm loved Dawn. Yes, the impulse
to worship is deep and ambiguous and old.

He was converted to biology at the age of sixteen at his
comprehensive by the new biology teacher who had come
straight from university, still looking so girlish that on her
first day she was mistaken by the caretaker for one of the
pupils. Most of the boys, Malcolm included, reckoned they
fancied her, and because she wore no ring on her finger their
fantasies seemed to contain the hope of fulfilment.

Just as older children have rites of initiation for the
nervous new kids, so the headmaster gave her all the worst
classes in the school, except for the Lower Sixth A-level
group upon which, relieved and liberated, she lavished her
enthusiasm for science which the other classes had evapor-
ated out of her through the apparatus of classroom disorder.

Thanks to Miss Curtis he went to university and became
a research scientist. Without her, he felt sure, that door
would have shut in his face. His dad used to say, 'Why go
messing with all that useless knowledge when with your brain
you could be out earning good money?'

Now, at the age of twenty-five, he wears on his lapel a metal badge which bears the symbol of a cross in a test-tube, the logo of the Christians in Science group. When asked about this he would zealously elaborate his favourite theme, eagerly withstanding the counter-blows of colleagues. 'Don't you think it is too reductive, too definitive – God in a test-tube, like a wasp caught in a jam-jar?' they would say. 'If I were God I would simply have to break out.' Inwardly there was part of him that accepted what they were saying. But it is one thing for God to break out, and another for one so conditioned as himself.

It goes without saying, of course, that his research project is experimental. He is trying to map the genes responsible for a certain type of auto-immune diabetes. If he succeeds it will be a small step forward in the understanding of that illness, and possibly as a result the lives of a small group of sufferers will be made more liveable. He apologises that the work is undramatic and not particularly high-tech, requiring patience and persistence, rather like being a stonemason working on a remote corner of a great cathedral. Yet for all its smallness in the great edifice of science, he sometimes flicks back his sandy hair and thinks, help, I am dealing with the basic building-blocks of our existence. Then he feels belittled, even humiliated, because the further he gets the more he discovers there is to know. It is awesome and frightening in a religious way. And they say it can only get worse as you grow older.

The impulse to worship is deep and ambiguous and old. Yes, Miranda was discovering that. She had come to Oxford like her father and mother before her, and seen it as her rightful inheritance. Her father had always talked of 'when you go to Oxford'. It was there for her use, her pleasure, her intellectual stimulation, her future, and she was so young, so attractive, so good at games, so good at the flute, so sexy, so much in demand. All this she celebrated by wearing golden lipstick, which earned her the nickname, at least amongst the more disreputable of her circle, Goldilicks. But the extravagant adventure of gifted youth can be a heavy burden to carry, and sometimes she wanted to receive from existence itself a great reassuring hug, confirmation that beneath all the exciting razzmatazz there was actually a cohesive meaning. But where should she look? It was not as if she was unique in this exceptional society, not as if her predicament stuck out a mile. There were plenty like her. Her parents had stressed self-sufficiency and resourcefulness as important values, and they had always discouraged her from religious allegiance, which they regarded as a sign of intellectual weakness and dependency. When Ali had suggested one morning, as they jogged back to college along Parks Road, that she should join her at what she referred to simply as The Prayer, it didn't seem such an absurd idea as a month ago it might.

Each day Malcolm walked to the lab from his room in north Oxford through the Parks. It is a place of goalposts and trees with Latin names, a place in which persons are requested to walk round the sports fields and to avoid making tracks and spoiling play. Spoilsports! Life is about making tracks. They are important. We need to know where others have been before, to recognise a successful route, to provide a map of how things might be done. A track can cut across convention, and this is exactly what the curators are complaining about. Cutting across the rugby field is a radical course that sometimes has to be taken. We must not be deceived by lines that hold no significance for us. This is one of the first lessons of research. However, the curators need not have feared about Malcolm because in this case he preferred not to take the shortest line from A to B, but to have time for reflection, contemplation. He would go down to the river which divides the park, muddy green and lethargic, indifferent to the prodding of punt poles, children playing Poohsticks or a dog retrieving its ball. Flowing across the centuries rivers are the symbols of timelessness, escape, forgetfulness, self-defence – on the south of the city the river was flooded during the Civil War to strengthen the defences. But if there was time he liked to go a quarter of a mile downstream where the river changes mood, and on a bright day the water that breaks over the weir is fragmented into seasurf, blue and white, sparkling, rushing with surprising force in such a flat land. You would sometimes see punters trying to navigate their craft across the whirling pool beneath the rollers from the upper to the lower river. Each time they push off from the bank they are driven round in a circle and back again to where they started. The situation is a model of more dramatic and dangerous wrestling with the elements at sea or in the rapids of a precipitous canyon, and the group of onlookers which has gathered on the bridge becomes a small crowd absorbed with the struggle, shouting encouragement, heckling, laying odds. And united in a common cause they lose their inhibitions and begin to discuss not only the plight of the navigators, but themselves.

But Malcolm liked the mornings best – their freshness was like a cool shower on a hot day. Just once a year when the leaves are golden, rusty brown, and frustrate the winter by refusing to fall, there'll be a misty morning with a sharp hoar-frost when there is a Christmassy echo in the air with leaves falling randomly, profusely, rhythmically as though the ice has cracked the last tenuous thread between stalk and stem. And as the trees snow down their golden flakes the canopy doesn't seem to diminish. It is a time of stasis, a suspension of time like a silent vigil before winter, and all of nature, birds and plants, the slow, forgetful river, bows in quiet reverence.

It was on such a morning that Malcolm found his reverie broken. Emerging through the mist along the path he saw a shape, a human figure, running, closing on him. Not plodding or staggering like so many bottom-heavy joggers, but streamlined, self-confident, jubilant in movement. She approaches more silent than the morning, yet stirring up a current which ruffled his stillness. Enthralled, he summons all his concentration to absorb as much of her as he can in the seconds available. Her brown hair is drawn back into a pony tail, her lips are luminously yellow with fashion make-up, which seems oddly inconsistent with the whole ethos of running for health and fitness, but it definitely accentuates what is a distinctively beautiful face, high-boned, blue-eyed, nose subtly asymmetric throwing all into a patrician perspective. She is wearing a personal stereo round her head, with the little ear-muff speakers emitting a noise so loud that he could hear for a moment the extraneous notes of what sounded like chanting. He wanted more time to behold her, wanted her to reappear again and again like the golden leaves that are falling around him, but as he turned, her agile frame dissolved into the mist.

Malcolm had decided that there were three ambiguities about his faith: (1) That which arose from the religion he had discovered with Dawn, traditional, conservative, puritanical. Although he had often wanted to break out of that mould, having experienced it at a very impressionable age, its cautions and restrictions ran deep. This was the ambiguity of tradition versus innovation. (2) The ambiguity forced upon him by his scientific method which said basically that no theory is sacred, everything is up for grabs and open to questions, perhaps even that there are no ultimate certainties. This was the ambiguity of the mind versus the heart. (3) And this was the worst of all, the ambiguity caused by all the desires that insinuate themselves between himself and God. Blessed are the pure in heart for they shall see God. Could anyone really see God, then? It seemed his fundamental spiritual problem, and he did not recognise that it was as old as the hills.

The small ad that had caught Malcolm's eye and drawn him to The Prayer claimed that here was a fresh approach to spirituality. Inside the church there was an aura of Eastern Orthodox solemnity: golden light of candles (hundreds of them in small glass tumblers, on the altar, on window-ledges, on the floor), icons in autumn shades, incantation. The simple chant, *Ubi caritas, Deus ibi est* – where there is love God is found – repeated over and over again, like a mantra, she later said, which he thought sounded sinister, like a praying mantis, until she explained that a mantra is a Hindu sacred text used as an incantation. A text taken from the Veda, the Hindu sacred writing. In principle, a perfectly non-judgemental comparison, but he was uncomfortable with the non-Christian implication. In the chapel students sat in the lotus position on a floor covered with coconut matting. A spine-curved youth with wiry red hair prays with an intonation betokening injury, submission, sadness. I am speaking to you, Lord, out of a sense of undeserved hurt. The group dynamic pulls people into corporate submission, their eyes closed, bodies gently swaying to the chanting. There comes a point when a collection of individuals all identified by the personal pronoun 'I', becomes 'us'. Is this losing yourself to find yourself, he wondered. Or has the self been subsumed into a greater, more monstrous corporate ego? Slowly the worship infiltrates the corporate soul in a way that creates such an air of 'this is right', that to criticise it would be like a sin against the Holy Spirit. We belong. We are empowered to define what is spiritual, what is appropriate. We need tracks, liturgical pathways that can lead us by the most direct route to God. But Malcolm felt himself pacing about in his own mind making space for paranoia. He could not match his temperament to this. He wanted, against all his scientific judgement, to write a notice: persons are requested to avoid making tracks and spoiling play.

Another guy, big-bodied, has prostrated himself completely so that his mouth seems to suck like a baby the dirt-trodden matting. Others, arriving late, step over the body. Amongst them are girls in high-heeled shoes and Burberry raincoats, who sit on the floor, backs hunched, but some beautifully vertical, splaying their legs. The leaders, who have been sitting on their haunches, do obeisance by bending their torsos to the ground like Muslims. They are leaves covering the cold earth. Then, in the crowd he sees the jogger, straight-backed, elegant of proportion, muscular, yellow waxen mouth in sensual prayer, and through the solemn stillness he feels a disturbing wind beginning to blow. Yes, the impulse to worship is deep and ambiguous and old.

Malcolm knelt in prayer, making repeated attempts at concentration, trying to get through to God, searching for that elusive purity of heart. But each time he found himself standing at the head of one of Oxford's narrow medieval streets, the kind of street where from their bedroom windows neighbours once conversed in complete privacy or eloped with one another across a plank. In fact the street is scaffolded now – they are painting the newly stuccoed gables in bright colours. Malcolm looks up and sees two figures who appear to be dancing. At first he can't make them out in the misty evening light, then their silhouettes edge into focus, like shadows projected on a sheet – a technique for entertainment and illusion. It is a man and a woman; he is kneeling and lifting his arms up to the sky, she stands on tiptoes reaching high, high as she is able, to pull silk scarves from the air, each arm, wrist and hand alternately plucking and circling down, and each time she conjures down new treasures, her beautiful straight back, like the hand of a clock, moves lower through the early minutes of the hour: five, six, seven, eight, nine, ten, eleven, twelve, thirteen, fourteen. They are the spirits of reaching and searching. They seek and find. His wiry hair has become strangely bright as he mimes his submission and his sadness. Now the woman reaches the minute of the quarter hour, her lips touch his and suddenly he is clothed in vermilion, red and emerald silk. He rises to embrace her with a passion unliturgical, and locked in lovers' arms they float away. But why? Why? Why does she bestow her precious nard on him?

A memory of childhood flashed across Miranda's mind from a time before her mother had died and her father had married again. It must have been one of those few Christmases with her mother that she was able to remember; there were real candles on the tree and underneath the lower branches a pile of presents wrapped in gold, and red, and ultramarine. Now as she sang *Ubi caritas*, her attention was fixed on the candle flames and their faint reflections which flickered on the icons as if in a cloudy mirror. The repetition of the chant – where there is love God is found – percolated slowly into her like melt water through a mountainside until it should emerge months, years later in a crystal-clear spring. She was aware that other people were present, but she felt free of them. She even felt free of herself, and of her own beautiful body, as if the alkali of holiness could somehow neutralise its chemical power. Who God was she was unclear, uncertain, but she felt that she was reaching out to something beyond herself through worship that cut across the touchlines of tradition as she had known it at school. This 'prayer' didn't even have a specific beginning or end; you could enter when you wanted and go before it stopped; there was no blessing or procession or paraphernalia. But there was dignity. That in a silly way was important.

When in the sixteenth century Copernicus examined and re-examined his astronomical data he had to force himself to believe the absurdity which it impelled him towards, that the planets including the Earth revolve elliptically around the Sun. It was hard to kick against the theology-encrusted theory that in fact truth was opposite, and he pinched himself to believe what he saw through the window. When, several decades later, Galileo supported the Copernican against the Ptolemaic theory, he was arrested for his blasphemy. You see our experiments are not simply ways of checking what we think might be true; they are windows through which, if we look carefully, we shall recognise truths that we had never thought of before. Reality can subvert all our theories, and we are fortunate when it does. We can be looking for one thing but find another.

Malcolm feared that his subconscious mind was guilty of blasphemy, by persistently wanting to cut a path across the field of play called worship, interposing images that grate against the repressive respectability of his religious upbringing. But in an unexpected way he was beginning to observe himself in prayer rather as he observed cells in the laboratory, carefully trying to avoid jumping to conclusions, or twisting evidence to support a pet theory.

Is it truly blasphemy to balk at the man-made symbolic structures, which so inadequately materialise our relationship with the divine? God's holiness is quite safe and needs no protection from us. If all the world said yahboo to God, his holiness would not be damaged one bit. The problem is that *we* need to protect the holiness of God for *ourselves*. We need to symbolise it because we have an insatiable desire to grasp the ungraspable, and we fear for the fragile quality of our union with God. Therefore we are irascible and touchy about any criticism of the lines we have drawn in our search for the ultimate truth. Blasphemy doesn't damage God, it endangers, we think, our possession of God's holiness.

George Steiner said that all great art has a touch of blasphemy to it. Perhaps one could say that all true religion has a touch of blasphemy to it. Besides the Jews believed that it was blasphemous to speak the name of God. It was too holy. But to begin to see God we have to name him, or try to name him, to experiment with the revelations that he gives us, shuffling and rearranging them, taking the way of the holy through the clumsy pass of trial and error. What is blasphemy, anyway? No one seems very sure these days. To look for God and see a beautiful woman? To speak disrespectfully of God? To undermine the dignity of God? To incite others to disrespect God? To speak disrespectfully of the Church, the Islamic culture, Judaism? Jesus was accused of blasphemy because he claimed to know God and he dared to criticise Pharisaic Judaism. In fact he couldn't have elucidated the truth without blaspheming, because he recognised new truths that undermined the fabric of the established religion.

Malcolm and Miranda were running in different directions. Maybe it was inevitable that they should bump into each other going the other way.

As people were drifting out, Malcolm lingered in the porch wondering whether he ought to go and talk to one of the clergy and ask for spiritual advice, or whatever one does. Some of the students were arranging to have breakfast together. 'Hey. I recognise you', said one of them. 'You're the guy who leered after me in the Parks.'

'No, no, I was genuinely . . .'

'Why not join us for breakfast?'

Later in his scientific notebook Malcolm wrote: 'The further you unwrap the truth the more awesome that truth becomes. We often say in science that the solution to a problem has great elegance. In other words it is awesomely beautiful in the simple way it reveals a truth about our universe. The same can be said of pathways to God. God must be revealed in ways that are awesomely beautiful in the simplicity of their message, because mystery is not what is hidden behind a screen or imagined in a dark corner – that is simply to admit that you are mystified. Mystery is the glorious vastness of reality. The more I learn the more I recognise I don't know. *Ubi caritas deus ibi est.*'

# Well, Here I Am . . .

Well, here I am writing these stories, if you call them stories.
I'm not quite sure what to call them: stories, parables, narrative reflections, encounters, watercolours, meditations. No,
not meditations. Meditations suggests something rather more
overtly religious than I am intending.

Well, here I am trying to write a bit about God, in
fragments, because that is how I meet him, in moments,
often unexpectedly. I sometimes wonder whether these are
the times when he chooses to disclose himself to me, or
whether they are the occasions when I am sufficiently in
tune with him for our relationship to take one of its erratic
jumps forward.

Could it even be that if I were to pick up all these odd-
shaped pieces, wherever I find them, and fit them together
like a jigsaw, I would have theology? You see what I am
trying to do is to escape from the self-regarding tunnel vision
of ecclesiastical institutions and the consolation-seeking spirituality that runs away from the world, and enter into the
incarnation. What do I mean by that? Perhaps that God is
where you least expect to find him.

The incarnation is really of fundamental importance to
my spiritual understanding, and what I understand it to
mean is that God is in the *world*, in the whole of it, in the
most unexpected places, and not merely in those parts of it
that we set apart and label 'holy'.

Have you ever thought that the problem with theology
might be that it spends far too little time asking the question
why, and far too much time writing in letters carved in
stone, all ending up with the grand statement – doctrines,
creeds, and liturgies? So, I am trying to write some parables,
which are probably far more churchy than they ought to be,
and in danger of disproving my theory! But those who seek
God must work with parables, because parables cross over

the boundaries of our experience, confronting you with the question of God, and who *you* are.

I would like you to have a look at this. Since I originally read it I have kept it printed out on a piece of paper somewhere in the piles of paper on my desk. I haven't framed it or anything because I don't go in for framing words.

'Children, only animals live in the Here and Now. Only nature knows neither memory or history. But man – let me offer you a definition – is the story-telling animal. Wherever he goes he wants to leave behind not a chaotic wake, not an empty space, but the comforting marker-buoys and trail signs of stories.' That's Graham Swift in *Waterland*. Definitely recommended reading.

Why do Christians have to divide themselves into opposing camps – in this case the 'certains' versus the 'questioners' – when in fact the stories on which our faith is based contain both assurance and questions? Anyone would think that conservatives never ask questions and liberals have no framework for what they believe. But surely both groups see God in what you might call the landmarks of his revelation, stories like Abraham, the Exodus, the Prophets, the Ministry of Jesus of Nazareth, his crucifixion, resurrection, and the coming of the Holy Spirit at Pentecost. These are the marker-buoys and trail signs which provide us with a map for faith.

However, it is sometimes forgotten that we have not lived through those events, we have discovered them by reading them second-hand in the narratives of the Bible. When they come to life, they do so only because our imaginations feed them with information from our own experience. For instance, how can we understand the power of Jesus' love on the cross unless we have some experience of the cost of love – pain, loss, the way the survival instinct resists acts of giving, wonder at the willingness of another person, probably a parent, to make a personal sacrifice for us?

Furthermore, in order to travel the roads and rivers that the map represents, it is necessary to read them in relation to the following questions: what do they mean to me? How do they gel with my experience? What do they mean to the world? And most important of all, how can we understand these stories in the light of issues such as violence, economics, starvation, conflicting cultural pressures, abuse of global resources, art, science, crime and punishment, and so on?

Because when Christian understanding has advanced most, the agenda has been set not by internal, ecclesiastical pressures, but by the attempt of Christians to respond to outside influences. Our stories help us to do that. Religious man – let me offer you a definition – is the story-telling animal.

So, I say to myself, beware of the grand statement. Don't let it trap you. You are not obliged to conform. Grand statement is the public face of theology, often the lowest common denominator of a wide variety of individual pictures of the nature of God, behind which lie the real guts of religious questioning.

I am sure too that there are many more Christians and would-be Christians than we imagine, all responding to the religious instinct, asking the questions why and how. In this sense theology is private and individual, millions of versions of it existing in the minds of millions of searchers, only now and then finding its way to the surface of public statement, each one painting a unique picture of the infinite God, and most humbly fearful that they have missed the truth, shy about letting on when experience hasn't matched up to the grand statements of creed and doctrine. Perhaps we should adapt Jesus' great maxim and say that doctrine was made for man and not man for doctrine. Theology is the servant of faith and not its master.

In the Carrick Roads, off Falmouth, where the sea, driven by wind and tides, cuts creeks through the green and cow-brown hills of Cornwall, I sometimes go sailing. I had lessons when I was thirty and therefore approach the task with all the self-conscious uncertainty of adulthood, not like the children who flex their backs to the sails and move in unity with the elements. Taut and excited I beat across the bay, stung by rainbow spray, astonished by the aerodynamics which permit me to move so swiftly into the wind. I could go to France, or through the treacherous Western Approaches past the Scillies to America. Could I? I am out of my depth, and go about to run with the wind, swanning and surfing back to the safety of the harbour, when a squall whips up from behind and smashes the boom across my head. I am in the water, not in a river creek but in the sea, and the capsized boat pitches and rolls with the waves, I am sure for a moment, away from me, out of my reach,

teasing me into a panic. When at last I right the boat
and heave my shock-shivering body aboard, I recognise the
admonishment of the wind. The phrase 'the wind bloweth
where it listeth' howls in my mind like the howling of the
rigging. Now I remember the rest of it: 'and you hear the
sound of it, but you do not know whence it comes or whither
it goes; so it is for everyone who is born of the Spirit'.

When I meet God, will he be frightening and exhilarat-
ing; as Sara Maitland puts it, 'wild, not tamed'?

Tomorrow I will go sailing again.

Well, here I am trying to write these stories and wondering
whether I ought to locate them for you on my own spiritual
map. But then this is not about tying up loose ends, is it. It
is about the wonder of exploring God in the unexpected . . .

One such exploration for me is always unexpected when
it happens, and it happened again last night. I returned after
a long break to prayer. Well, to be precise, a particular kind
of prayer with God which seems to me deeper and more
personal than anything I am used to in my daily prayers at
the eucharist. Not that I mean for one moment to diminish
the liturgy with its rhythm, its shape, its drama, and its
gratefully accepted discipline. But I had been reviewing a
book about the writings of Don Cupitt and found a part of
my mind supporting his claim that religious response has
nothing to do with any external reality. So it was interesting
that that old sensation of prayer should come flooding back
as soon as I lay my head down on the pillow.

I feel like I imagine artists must feel when after a long
period of struggling with a canvas a happy accident occurs
and the painting suddenly comes to life. In fact, I associate
the two experiences so closely that I think of prayer as
essentially creative.

Silence is like looking at a pond and saying, 'There is
water'. But when you fish out a jam-jar full of the water
you see it contains millions of organisms, and each organism
contains cells and millions of atoms. You look at the surface
of the pond, calm and rippled, and you say, 'Isn't water
restful'.

This is the silent land where one step forward leaves self
behind, where the sea shell echoes the whispering music of
communication across the spheres, a silence in which to wait,

like the silence of night in a place remote from all the roar and rumble of distant roads. A silence of confidence and candour, able to absorb and comprehend the incoherent searchings of the mind.

All silence has its sounds: a note played by the wind, the rain dripping outside an open window, your own breath. In this land I hear the sound of irrefutable righteousness evaluating my motives sympathetically, but searchingly, person to person. Like in Psalm 139, there is no escape: 'If I dwell in the uttermost parts of the sea, even there thy hand shall lead me'.

The inescapability of God doesn't worry me, though, because there is both judgement and support. I like to think of the world embedded in God, rather than a God who is outside and who from time to time intervenes in human affairs. I don't think this is a picture entirely alien to Jesus', 'Our Father who art in heaven'. It is complementary. In the book of Deuteronomy there is a sentence which is used at the beginning of the funeral service, 'The eternal God is your refuge and underneath are the everlasting arms'. The world is enwrapped in the great loving hug of God. You can just see God standing there like a colossus, holding the world in his arms and feeling the weight of it, thinking to himself, I wish I could put this down.

I think I prefer the more abstract picture which Paul provides of a God 'in whom we live and move and have our being'. This changes several perceptions in prayer. For example, one no longer calls on God as one who comes in from outside – you are living *in* God. Nor is God like a divine political commentator, with an overview of world affairs. All world events are in God, and sin and evil destroy the equilibrium of God, break up the balance of his being, frustrate his purposes. And instead of calling out to God, stretching out your hands, you must ask God to tune you in to his being. It is like the body with its mechanisms for disposing of damaged cells and replacing them with healthy ones.

I often feel guilty that these happy accidents of prayer do not occur more often. Or rather, I experience a feeling of immense relief when they do because my Christian discipleship would, I think, disintegrate if I did not from time to time think that God had an objective reality with which I was able to communicate.

The lesson of the silence is to accept the images it creates, the sounds that belong to it, however odd they seem,
but not say to yourself, 'Right, now I have it. This is it.
Let me take my chisel and write this down.' Next time it
will be different. God is too immeasurable to be written
down.

So here I am writing these stories, and I thought you
would like to know a little more about. . . .

# Emmaus

The story of the Road to Emmaus unravels the secret of the resurrection. Two followers of Jesus are making a journey, and as they walk they discuss the dramatic circumstances of their Master's sudden execution, when Jesus joins them. But they do not recognise him. That in itself is extraordinary, surely. How could they not recognise him? Either they were in such a state of shock and confusion that they were not really with it. Or there was something quite different about the Risen Lord. I go for the second explanation, not least because failure to recognise the Risen Lord is characteristic of most of the gospel resurrection stories. For example, in the garden cemetery Mary sees Jesus and thinks he must be the gardener; on the Galilean shore the disciples who have returned to their fishing do not know who it is who tells them to cast their net on the other side of the boat; and even in the closed room, when he appears, they do not recognise him until he shows them the wounds in his hands.

The Stranger on the road then expounded the scriptures to explain how they pointed to the coming of Christ, and you notice how the emphasis is not on resurrection but on suffering. Because it is in the suffering of Christ that the secret of new life is to be found. Just as three years before in the synagogue he had expounded the text from Isaiah, 'The spirit of the Lord is upon me because the Lord has anointed me to bring good tidings to the afflicted', perhaps now he spoke of Isaiah's picture of the suffering servant, a man of sorrows who was bruised for our iniquities. And how the sacrifice of all selfishness reveals the true nature of eternal life and what potential it has. This is the point, as I argued earlier, that Mark makes so powerfully in his Gospel by not including any resurrection stories. What further proof do you need of eternal life? You have seen it in the manner of Jesus' life and death, and as Jesus said himself, those who obstinately refuse to open themselves to God would not believe even if one were to rise from the dead.

Eventually, when the disciples persuade the Stranger to stay and eat with them, they recognise him at the moment that he breaks the bread, says a blessing, and shares it with them. This could not be a more explicit reference to the eucharist, and to the practice of the early Church of commemorating the Lord's Supper – a theme which permeates the gospel material. It reminds us of other eucharistic occasions like the beach barbecue after the disciples had hauled in their freak catch of fish – 153 of them. Or the Feeding of the Five Thousand and the boy's five barley loaves and two small fishes. It is not surprising that the fish became a symbol for Christ, and is frequently found in the catacombs in combination with bread and wine as an emblem of the eucharist.

In other words these resurrection stories are bursting with symbolism and cross-reference. They do not stand as a separate testimony to a rather strange and peculiar interim state of affairs called the 'Resurrection', a time between Easter morning and the Ascension, but interlock with all the other gospel material, demonstrating that the resurrection is inseparable from the rest of the story, and belongs intimately to it. Perhaps that is why the Third Eucharistic Prayer of the Anglican Liturgy (ASB Rite A) says that 'Christ revealed the resurrection by rising to new life'. He revealed something that already existed.

The Road to Emmaus is also a parable for our own Christian pilgrimage, a kind of Pilgrim's Progress, which leads you from the confusing bustle of Jerusalem, along a dusty track through rocky terrain until you arrive outside the town and see in the distance its roofs and walls climbing like great stairs across the hillside, pink and radiant in the evening sun, shaded by palms and trellises of grape-vines. Along the road you discuss the puzzling, often mind-boggling, questions of God and faith. You like to talk about it, discuss it. You need to do that, to exchange ideas, and swap experiences – without holding back or feeling shy. Some of your views will be unorthodox, and you need not be ashamed of them. The Holy Spirit's purpose in leading you into faith is to lead you into reality, not to make you kid yourself, or tie yourself up in mental contortions, so that when you are confronted by common-sense critics you have to become a theological Houdini. There is too much of that, as if it were a virtue to make ourselves believe the incredible. What is orthodoxy, anyway, but a general consensus of what constitutes the norm of Christian teaching. We have too many hang-ups about what is right to believe. The clergy are the worst, especially when we spy another dog-collar in the congregation. Frantically we flick through our sermon notes and wonder, have I got my theology right on such and such a point, as if there were a right answer to what we are trying to get across, instead of many different ways of approaching a religious idea. Or indeed, which is worse, as if the congregation were not able to discern sense and nonsense in our sermons anyway.

So, as we tread the road, we are tempted to hide our doubts and questions from each other, and then we hide them from ourselves, suppress them. Whereas if we were more open with each other, we would enlighten one another, and build up each other's faith. No other discipline despises the process of trial and error, or the questioning of received doctrines, the sifting and sorting of experience, so why should Christianity?

After discussion, Jesus is known in the breaking of bread. Not every Christian will think of heaven or resurrection or new life being contained in the eucharist, with all its conventional mannerisms, ancient and modern. Some are turned off by music of previous centuries, others by the stylised bonhomie of shaking hands or kissing at the peace. And yet the liturgy has a magnetism that draws people back. It provides historical continuity, and can transcend the trivialities of changing fashion. Above all it is a model for new life, a dramatic representation of a wider experience, the experience of relationship, celebration, necessity, hunger, offering, self-giving. But just as the eucharistic pictures in the New Testament are many and varied (I never mentioned St John and the Water into Wine, or the Woman at the Well, and the accompanying speeches of Jesus which begin 'I am the True Vine' and 'I am the Bread of Life', did I), so our eucharistic experience reaches beyond the Sunday-morning slot into the everyday. I often think that we get nearer to the secret of the eucharist in entertaining one another at home, especially in those spontaneous invitations to people we scarcely know.

Or in going to the Wimpy and sitting down to a cheese-burger with someone who has stopped you in the street to ask for food.

There is one other feature of the Road to Emmaus story which deserves special attention: the disciples asked the Risen Lord to eat with them *before* they knew who he was. They were generous and hospitable without any base motive. They simply had not realised it was Christ whom they invited. Afterwards they might have recalled the words of Jesus on another occasion, Inasmuch as you do it to the least of these my brethren, you do it unto me. No one conveys that truth more powerfully than Leo Tolstoy in his story of the devout cobbler who wished to meet Christ and was promised one night at his prayers that he would do so the next day. As he worked at his street-level bench mending shoes he watched the world go by, and saw the sadness of the human predicament. There was a snow-sweeper, raw with cold, whom he invited in for a moment to warm himself. There was a mother with her child, a thin weakly creature, under-nourished and poorly clothed. He called them in and gave the woman a cloak and the child some food. Later in the day an old woman was robbed of the fruit she had brought to the market, and the cobbler ran to her aid. That night in prayer he challenged God: you promised that I would meet Christ today, but he hasn't come. Then out of the shadows appeared the three characters, each one saying, 'I am he'.

The heart of the resurrection is found here. Such stories give us the clue as to how we can meet Jesus and walk with him on the road and bring new meaning to our encounter with him in the breaking of bread.

# Holy Innocents' Day

Alan left his wife just after Christmas because he couldn't cope with their childlessness any longer. On Christmas Day he and Chris had been to deliver the presents to his sister's kids, and to coo over the new baby. Flavia was a rather pretentious name for a baby, he thought, but that was his sister all over. It went with the Surrey house and the big Mercedes which Roger wouldn't have chosen, but had to drive to impress his clients. They also had an 'ozone-friendly' runabout in the garage. Chris thought she might have exorcised the baby obsession by now, but of course she hadn't. Most of the afternoon she cuddled 'Flia' while Alan, Roger and the boys played upstairs. It was when she felt the delicate, gummy mouth nuzzling at her blouse that the despair returned, and the tears began to well. She could even imagine herself as one of those baby-snatchers lurking outside a supermarket.

The electric railway in the loft was a classic; the GWR re-created. Cuttings, tunnels, bridges, mail bags, milk churns, every detail, recalled the great days of the steam era. Roger had assembled it at nights throughout the autumn, unveiled it at five o'clock that morning, and now, its chief executive, drank its health in a continuous toast of champagne. While Adam and Tobias, the bedazzled and inquisitive new owners, suffered the indignity of being told to be careful, or not to touch. 'But it is ours, Daddy', they protest.

'Chris is looking broody', says Roger through the champagne haze. 'Isn't it about time you did something about it, old boy?'

On the Boxing Day they had decided to stay in and have their own Christmas at home, à deux. They got up late, there wasn't much else to do, and Chris was in one of her moods. She came down in her dressing-gown and slumped back in an armchair looking out of the window. It was one

118

of those blank, cold, but frostless days, in the wet decrepitude of the December garden. She gazed at the nail-rusted fencing, gapped and crooked, and saw ugly, voracious teeth. He made coffee, busied himself in the kitchen, put on a record of Christmas music from King's, or somewhere like that, proposed a drive into Hertfordshire to see the hunt, all in a concerted attempt to save the day.

An hour later she said, 'I hate your bloody sister and her complacent bloody motherhood'.

'Please. Let's not go through that again.'

'I hate bloody Christmas – "Unto us a child is born" – it's not true. What is Christmas without children? Just a chance for people like your sister to get all weepy and sentimental about their precious offspring.'

'For goodness sake, Chris. It's no good moping. There are other things in life, more important things, more interesting things, and in our situation we've got to go out and find them.'

He resented her emotion. When all the tests failed to give encouragement, he had repressed hopes of fatherhood, and hidden them underneath the book he was going to write, and the car he was going to restore. The medics simply couldn't solve the problem. For six years they had dragged themselves in and out of clinics, including that of a Harley Street specialist, but they always kept their infertility a secret from friends and relations. Don't give them the chance to patronise or be sorry for us, was Chris's attitude. Deep down they both blamed each other. Until this recent depression Chris always wanted to make him talk, talk, talk. And he wanted to make her shut up, shut up, shut up.

It was the hopeless emptiness of that Boxing Day afternoon that made him decide he had had enough. It seemed as though their relationship had shed its last leaf, and although underneath the bare branches there was still love, he didn't believe that it could ever rise into another spring. Perhaps they would find other partners. Perhaps with someone else . . . Perhaps with someone else their seed would blossom and flourish. So three days later he walked out on his wife and 52 Hallfield Road.

What made Alan enter the church hall having seen the unenticing poster that dank January night is not certain.

Perhaps it was because he hadn't talked with anyone for a week, except to tell the bed-and-breakfast lady whether he wanted tomatoes with his bacon and fried bread. It was still the holidays, so he hadn't been into school, either, but wandered the streets and the January sales in the vicinity of his school, three stations up the line from home.

'How very good to see you', said the shiny-nosed man with a raincoat over his cassock. A trickle of people, most of them elderly, most apprehensive. The vicar's enthusiastic handshake held Alan tight, while his eyes darted across, beside, around, unwilling to miss the next hand to wring.

'Thank you. I'm Alan Wordsworth.'

'Now let me see', he said, screwing up his eyebrows as if he ought to know. 'Which church do you belong to?'

'I wouldn't say that I belong to any church exactly, although I sometimes worship at St Peter's. I've rather fallen from grace recently – a little less certain of the ultimate truths, stumbling round on the edge of mysteries.' Alan laughed a rather truncated laugh that he never intended to come out.

'Well, there's a cup of tea at the refectory.' The vicar pointed towards a kitchen serving-hatch that reminded Alan of his school canteen, except that here the ladies were not of the couldn't-care-less dolloping sort, but wore smart suits and made jolly conversation.

'You must excuse me. How very good to see you, Mrs Wedderspoon', said the vicar, diverted by another pastoral concern. 'Yes, it is good that we are here', thought Alan, recalling an assembly he had taken on the Feast of the Transfiguration.

It was the Warnock Committee of 1984 on human fertilisation and embryology that must be blamed for this. Were the scientists, experimenting with ova and sperms and embryos, cultured in a test tube, planning by quality control to develop a master race? When is a human being not a human being? Is it murder to allow a fertilised female egg to multiply its cells, study it, and then wash it down the sink? There was a spate of meetings in churches and church halls to discuss what had become a topical area for moral debate. How many church-goers really had troubled consciences about these issues is not clear, except, Alan suspected, that the number was small. But it became a fashionable subject in church circles, of the kind that every vicar who desires to be up to the minute feels he must have a meeting about.

The hall on that chilly night was warmed in its hollow spaciousness by gas fires suspended half-way up the wall. They peered down beneath the blue-barrelled ceiling like tepid suns creating pools of tolerable comfort in which people congregated. On the wooden cornice that ran the circumference of the hall where the curved ceiling met the walls was a dust-encrusted shuttlecock leaning precariously over. It suddenly occurred to Alan that he was drinking his cup of tea on the base line of the badminton court, and that the green canvas tubular chairs had been set out in a semi-circle on the opposing service courts. How odd, he thought to himself, that church halls always seemed to display these sporting icons when their occupants appear to be beyond the age of active participation. Did the vicar, who wore his raincoat against the uncertain warmth, come here on other nights in other attire, white socks and tennis shoes, to thrash a shuttlecock backwards and forwards until it became stranded on that upper ledge? How would tonight's discussion avoid ending up the same way?

Alan was standing alone, on the base line, in the ritual preliminaries of refreshments, when suddenly he turned to read the notices on the back wall – 'Starting next term the price of orange squash at the playgroup will be increased to 15p. Mothers . . .'. He was hoping that she hadn't seen him. But there she was, the school lollipop lady, a queenly apotheosis of dumpiness crowned by a brimmed green felt hat with what looked like cherries appended to the side. Everyone seemed to know Mrs Wright and she seemed to know you, making you her business. There were those who thought her fierce, but children liked her, and she had a reputation for moral rectitude, sharpened by an old-fashioned London accent which had migrated from the Kingsland Road to Palmers Green. To add to this largely unwarranted image of severity, she had a son called Ron, a gentle fellow who lived at home with mum and worked as a gardener in a local park. 'Here comes Mrs Wright and Ron', they would say. And then they would giggle.

'Hello, Mr Wordsworth. What are you doing here?'

'I might ask you the same question, Mrs Wright.'

'You know me, dear, I come to all these dos.'

'But I wouldn't have thought infertility and embryo experiments were quite up your street.'

'Go on with you, Mr Wordsworth. I might not be as young as I used to be, but when it comes to babies I know a thing or two. I had four myself, you know – all at home. And I don't hold with all this messing about. I told Reverend Walters, I did, the Church must speak out against it.'

I'm sure this wasn't meant as a provocation, but there was a hint of umbrage in his voice. 'They take a female ovum, Mrs Wright, when it is ripe, from the would-be mother's ovaries, by a surgical method known as laparoscopy, and introduce the male sperm to it in a small glass dish. If a sperm manages to break through the wall of the female cell and fertilise it, then that cell divides, and the divided cells divide, and so on. Those few cells are scarcely visible to the eye. The process is at first very remote from babies.'

'Come on, Mr Wordsworth, you're not in the classroom now. Anyway, you're an English teacher, aren't you? How do you know so much about it?' Alan took her arm in a confidential manner, dislodging her hat with his shoulder and causing her to spill tea in her saucer. He stooped towards her ear.

'I've been inside one of the laboratories and seen it all. Why do you think I haven't got any kids myself?'

'None of my business, dear. I know you young people have your mortgages and things. Kids come later.'

'No, it isn't that. We want . . . we wanted children. We've tried for them. But we don't seem to be able to.' He smiled defensively and began to believe he had been too frank.

'Oh I am sorry, dear.'

'Please, don't be sorry. There's nothing wrong with Chris and me.' (At least, not physically, he thought. Just the small matter of the complete breakdown of our relationship. That's all.) 'I mean we're not ill. In fact they say that there's no physical reason why we can't have a baby, except that we both produce antibodies that make conception more difficult than it would otherwise be.'

My God, why tell this to Mrs Wright of all people? Their – his – private life will be public property. What will she think when he crosses the road in the morning? Good morning Mr Wordsworth. (There's the man with the antibodies.) Will she look him in the face again? Or will her eyes be drawn inevitably down towards the source of his ineffectualness?

No, Mrs Wright, you don't understand. Yet for the first time he had confessed, owned up, to someone who wasn't a medic. Here he was, after a week of loneliness which he had dragged across pavements, into cinemas, and through municipal parks to the point of ragged exhaustion, disclosing his secrets to the first person who speaks to him, who happens to be the redoubtable Mrs Wright. After all she does seem to be a woman of the world, experienced. She ought to understand. So he regaled her with details that could never have been discussed with male friends, who would be embarrassed, and conditioned by the bravado of pub talk. He felt so much lighter for it. Why could Chris not do the same, instead of this silly 'I shall not be mocked' pact that she kept with herself? She ought to confide in her female friends. They would surely be full of encouragement, those friends who must have asked questions, hoped for her to join their exclusive club and be initiated into the mysteries of the missed period, the sickness, the slow swelling of womb and breasts, the fascinated glances of men in the street, the rosy ripe complexion, the fullness, the completeness of womanhood.

'I don't mean to embarrass you, Mrs Wright.'

'Don't worry, dear. I'm not embarrassed. These things aren't embarrassing. Life, I always say, is not embarrassing. I might not approve, but I don't blush.' She laughed proudly. 'In the blitz, you know, I worked in a hospital down Mile End, and it was my job to help with them that was injured, men and women. Sometimes there were bits of clothes blasted right into the skin, and no bomb, I can tell you, respects a person's privacy. Ever since then it has taken a lot to make me blush.'

The vicar struck the table with a spoon, calling the meeting to order, his voice part liturgical part auctioneer, the result no doubt of a long career in announcing hymn numbers. Alan shuffled to the back row with all the others – ladies, walking-sticks, duffel coats – in a slow-motion game of musical chairs.

The first speaker was introduced. There would be others, but perhaps none so providential. Up stood an orbicular-faced priest, much younger than Mrs Wright would have expected, a teacher of ethics from a seminary, his black garb and creased brow like a visual aid for the gravitas of what he was about to say. 'Brothers and sisters' – yes, he actually said that – 'I am concerned about life in all its many wonderful manifestations.' And the particular wonderful manifestation was, of course, the human embryo in the first fortnight of its existence. This life is not a potential human being, but a human being with potential and therefore it must necessarily be afforded the status of a human being. A human being with potential. Pause, to look around the audience. It is not good enough, he admonished, to think of children as goods that roll off the factory production line, subject to quality control, where only the fit-for-marketing survive. (Do any of us think of them like that?) Besides, the fundamental purpose of marriage is the procreation of children, for the increase of mankind according to the will of God. And it was the will of God that such increase should result from the physical act of union. It cannot be clear . . . It cannot be clear that children conceived without that physical act are willed by God. To put it another way, the connection between procreation and personal sexual contact should not be severed. (Except, supposed Alan, in the case of the miraculous conception of Jesus by Mary of the Holy Spirit.) The priest was suggesting that husband and wife should gratefully accept the will of God in this matter, whether a child is conceived or not. For example, many parents graciously accept the givenness of the situation, even when their child is handicapped. Experience suggests, does it not, that the eternal qualities of love and compassion are usually more deeply understood as a result of making sacrifices within a relationship than looking for an easy way out. And this is precisely what so many parents with a handicapped child have discovered, and what childless couples ought to recognise and accept.

Or again, consider this. While infertility has many morally neutral causes, it cannot be denied that *in vitro* fertilisation is often used to circumvent problems caused by previous abortion, the use of intra-uterine contraception, and sexually transmitted disease. Indeed, to sum up, God did not intend for babies to be conceived in glass dishes, and the fact that couples are prepared to spend such large sums of money for this kind of infertility treatment degrades the natural beauty of conception and reduces the procreation of children to the same moral and aesthetic plane as the January sales, which some of us will have been taking advantage of this week.

Mrs Wright joined in the applause with great vigour, stirred by the priest's rhetoric. But throughout the hall enthusiasm, like the heat, was patchy. Alan rose to his feet, clutching the back of the chair in front of him, so that the zip of his anorak clinked against the metallic frame. 'I would like to make an observation, if I may.'

Faces shocked and surprised turned on him, as if he had committed some horrible, unexpected crime. 'Sit down', commanded a blimpish voice. 'There will be a time for questions later', said the chairman.

What I have to say, continued Alan, adrenalin-confident, relates so closely to what the last speaker has said that I must say it now. (More shouts of wait, and sit down.) The Reverend Father idealises the sexual act in marriage, to the point of sentimentality. But that, I think, is common, even understandable, amongst those who have no direct personal experience of it – they either think of it as effortlessly beautiful or sufficiently awesome to defy serious thought. I suppose if you will draw the absurd parallel between marriage and Christ's sacramental relationship with his Church then all the mess and the failure has to be left out.

My wife and I have trudged to and from a fertility clinic at odd times, across Hampstead Heath early on frosty mornings, through the traffic jams of a humid summer evening at the behest of the menstrual cycle and the delicate, magical time of ovulation, because we want a baby, a child to love and nurture, to fulfil those insistent parental longings, that capacity for love that God has placed within us. We have learned more and more about the slippery reluctance of fertilisation, and nature's wasteful prodigality in battling to achieve it: the importance of diet, the hormone levels, the psychosomatic powers of temperament, the ovum repelling the attentions of millions of sperm, the one in ten chance of an embryo actually embedding in the wall of the uterus, the body's chemistry deciding to abort at any danger signal. We have wondered at the miracle of creation against such odds, and understood the uniqueness of each new birth; we have sacrificed personal dignity, knowing a sense of dispossession but not of shame, in order to bring our seed together. On one occasion we made an embryo – all eight cells of it – and when it was implanted in my wife I felt the pride of incipient fatherhood. I skipped round the park, made plans. People looked at me and recognised, I felt sure, the maturity of a progenitor, no longer a mere youth.

When my wife's period came as usual we were both devastated, didn't want to go out, or meet people, contemplated a barren future. But I never felt resentful that other people had children, or enjoyed them. The gift of life is too great to resent it.

What I say to you is that the sabbath was made for man and not man for the sabbath. Your morality, for all its concern for the dignity of human life, strikes me as hard and inhuman. Why should the Church be angry with my wife and me for using the skills of science to share with God in his work of creation, and for suffering in the act of creation? Or angry with scientists who push out the frontiers of knowledge both theoretically and experimentally. Are they Frankensteins of evil intent? Doesn't the crucifixion itself show us that creative love, even for God, is not given with effortless ease, but at great personal cost? And what is born of pain, whether pain of the body or pain of the spirit, is going to be cherished all the more greatly.

The hall was silent, as if waiting for him to continue. The people on the platform looked at him, attentive, interrogative, compassionate. They would have listened to more, but, suddenly in their faces Alan imagined he saw his wife looking down. He heard her crying, 'Why did you never let me see into the secrets of your soul like you have exposed it to these people?'

He turned to leave the hall and heard behind him his own footsteps resonant on the wooden floor, larger than life. What had he been saying? My wife and I . . . My wife . . . us. But he had left his wife, yet spoken of togetherness. What had spurred his anger and driven him to hold the floor, refusing to be silenced? It was that the priest had done to him what he, Alan, had done to his wife. He had belittled the dignity of his action, undermined the integrity of his emotion, told him it didn't matter, and given him nothing in its place. He had squeezed God out of the very places he needed to be.

Down the High Street the shop lights and neon signs reflected on the wet pavement and he saw his own image fragmented among them. He was aware of cars swashing by, leaving behind them a nonchalant spray that quickly settled into the vacant night. They had somewhere to go. A lone eater was crouched over something and chips in the Wimpy, observed by a bored waitress wearing a ridiculously comic cap. This was a far country and he was emotionally spent. He would take the tube, turn left, then right into Hallfield Road, and hope to God that she was still there.

# Fireworks

Who should have the last word? Giuseppe, Leandro, Joey?
One of the risk-taking eccentrics? I would like them all to
have the last word – I think each of them would have
something telling to say. Or Patsie, whom you haven't met?
Perhaps it ought to be her. You haven't met her because
she's been locked away and doesn't appear in public any
more, only writes letters, hundreds of them.

She was like a woman possessed before they took her
off. Completely dotty, and doubly dangerous. It was the fires,
you see. Pentecost Patsie. Her hair was like tongues of fire,
flaming orange with flickering curls licking upwards in ring-
lets, and her face ashen, powdered and ghostly, as if masked
permanently in one of those mud-packs. Mad Patsie should
have the last word. If she was in the Bible she would simply
have taken it for herself anyway. She would be one of those
possessed by evil spirits who would come punning and jumping out of the tombs to Jesus, and immediately recognise
what others have failed to see: I know thee who thou art,
the Holy One of God.

Or if she was in Shakespeare she would be the Fool,
Lear's Fool perhaps, the only one able to get away with
speaking the truth to the King without getting banished. At
once acutely sane and pathetically childish, Patsie is more
childish than a china doll, and like Matilda she plays with
matches. When you read her zany, schizoid, word-association
letters she speaks with all the uninhibited truthfulness of a
child. It is as if she were sitting with you on a bus and
saying in a loud voice, Mummy, why is that man so wrinkly?
Or, Mummy, why has that lady got a hairy chin? Except
when she speaks she is speaking to you.

She would come rushing up to me in church, and set
me up in front of other people. 'I need to know about the
Holy Spirit', she would say. 'Give me a tutorial on the Holy

Spirit. Tell me everything you know about the Holy Spirit.'
Before they were used to it people would stand there all
agog waiting for the secrets of the Kingdom of heaven to
pour forth, waiting for me to answer the question they had
never dared ask, and I would say, 'Well, er . . .' and then
she'd laugh. 'You must know something.' So she would try
another approach. 'I want to light the fire of Jesus in you.
Go on, Brian, let me light the fire of Jesus in you. It won't
hurt.'

Like a Shakespearian Fool there is a deep personal
sorrow beneath her ironic humour. It is the sorrow of living
in a world which seems to engulf her in hostility and she is
frightened, terrified, of being left alone. The paradox is that
while she is shrewd and cutting, irreverent and mocking, she
is a dependant who would say 'Nuncle . . . take the Fool
with thee'.

But now, as I say, she no longer appears in public.
'Pyromania' is the official reason – as she would say 'wild,
pentecostal ardour. What is wrong with that?' But really, of
course, she is lighting beacons and sending up distress rock-
ets so that we can see where she is. Now we all know exactly
where she is she writes letters.

Let me see if I can remember or recreate a typical letter.
It is the one about the Fall and the possibility of salvation.
At least, I think that's what it is. You'll see that she writes
a kind of poetry.

Hi Bri

Did Adam and Eve have one long picnic then?
I imagine she ribbed her husband like crazy
But I guess they got their passion fruit from God
Well they were of no race or class were they
Probably farmers or living in a leisure centre.
Was the garden like a Butlins. Redcoats and girls?
I bet they were by the sea. I bet it was
a desert island in the sun with palm trees and fish etc.
God made the firmament didn't he
And the sun and the moon by night and lots of stars
I saw the Hollywood film of the
Garden of Eden. It looked like an Amazon jungle.
Adam was a bit like Tarzan and Eve a bit like Jane.
They were going to film all the Bible but it was a flop
And very expensive, Sir.

You see if you've got credentials like Adam and Eve
it's OK and people are interested in you
But if you go to the Job Centre
you can't always get a job.
I got a job once from a job centre in Woodford Green
Let's call the Garden of Eden Woodford Grin.
I think you could do one of your very expensive mind
sermons about it.
I enjoy expensive mind sermons and put
a fiver in the collection.

I see no reason to judge Adam and Eve
or condemn God's creation.
I don't like condemning people.
I condemn their kids though.
Have you ever read the novel *Cain and Abel* from Hollywood.
I don't ever want to be in the USA for fear of crimes of money.
John P. got his wallet stolen in New York and
on their dollars it says 'In God we Trust'.
I don't trust in money. Lots of money is worry worry worry
where your next 1p is coming from
So God says share my food, feed my sheep
and offer food, shelter and clothing.
You see no one asks people to be tramps
yet if they come to the vicarage
they get turned away, don't they.
I could be a tramp if it wasn't for the canal.
There will always be the poor, Jesus says,
because people are selfish, unsocial, greedy people
and do not obey his commands of sharing bread and wine
and money and goods fairly.
Yet of course Jesus doesn't see why people have to be poor –
I come to give you life in abundance.
Jesus wants us to be civil and if possible
to get a good job in harvesting something
whether people or goods
He says – Let the children come unto me.

Once in church you said
'I believe; help thou mine unbelief'
and you looked very poorly and sad
so I wondered if you had lost your faith
and mind and courage and sanctity.
Yet of course God can soothe you
and believe in your talents
in your future and bring love to you
which is what he is all about, Sir.
God is about love. God is love.

# Fireworks

Praise him, Praise him
All ye little children
He is love
He is love
(my first hymn)
I sang it before my eyes were opened.

I'm writing this in the dark.
Are you scared of the dark?
I'm scared of your church. It's huge.
I'm not scared of Moses and
I'm not scared of dying
yet I am scared of doctors and nurses, and the Pope.
I'm scared of your dog. She's bigger than me.
I'm scared of my bosses and the churchwardens and
other people's tongues and straight talkers –
Very frightening.
I'm not scared of the loony do-gooders you get in church,
yet I am scared of war and bombs and Hitler.
People are often scarey, and scared.
But I'm not scared of Holy Communion any more.
I used to be but I'm not now.
I'm absolutely scared of life without love, though, Sir.

Bye bye for now.
Patsie

PS Light a candle for me –
   if you don't think it will be too dangerous.